U.S.—Japanese
Economic Relations

Pergamon Policy Studies on U.S. and International Business

Related Titles

PERGAMON POLICY STUDIES ON U.S. AND INTERNATIONAL BUSINESS

U.S.–Japanese Economic Relations
Cooperation, Competition, and Confrontation

Edited by
Diane Tasca

Study Directors
Zygmunt Nagorski
Masahisa Naitoh

Published in cooperation with
The Lehrman Institute

Pergamon Press
NEW YORK • OXFORD • TORONTO • SYDNEY • FRANKFURT • PARIS

Pergamon Press Offices:

U.S.A	Pergamon Press Inc., Maxwell House, Fairview Park, Elmsford, New York 10523, U.S.A.
U.K.	Pergamon Press Ltd., Headington Hill Hall, Oxford OX3 0BW, England
CANADA	Pergamon of Canada Ltd., 150 Consumers Road, Willowdale, Ontario M2J 1P9, Canada
AUSTRALIA	Pergamon Press (Aust) Pty. Ltd., P.O. Box 544, Potts Point, NSW 2011, Australia
FRANCE	Pergamon Press SARL, 24 rue des Ecoles, 75240 Paris, Cedex 05, France
FEDERAL REPUBLIC OF GERMANY	Pergamon Press GmbH, 6242 Kronberg/Taunus, Pferdstrasse 1, Federal Republic of Germany

382.0952
un 3

87820

Library of Congress Cataloging in Publication Data
Main entry under title:

U.S.-Japanese economic relations.

(Pergamon policy studies)
"Papers grew out of a series of monthly seminars,
held at the Lehrman Institute from October, 1978 to
May, 1979."
Bibliography: p.
Includes index.
1. United States—Foreign economic relations—Japan—
Addresses, essays, lectures. 2. Japan—Foreign economic
relations—United States—Addresses, essays, lectures.
I. Tasca, Diane. II. Lehrman Institute.
HF1456.5.J3U555 1980   382'.0952'073   79-26315
ISBN 0-08-025129-3

Printed in the United States of America

The opinions expressed in the following essays represent the personal views of their authors and should not be interpreted as the official positions either of the organizations with which they are affiliated or of The Lehrman Institute.

Contents

Introduction

The title of this collection could be regarded as a starkly simplified recapitulation of the postwar history of economic relations between Japan and the United States. The spirit of cooperation that marked these relations during the era of Japan's postwar recovery and emergence as a full participant in the international arena was qualified and checked by Japan's very success in competing with the United States in both the global and the American marketplace. And this competition has given rise to increasingly troubled confrontations between the two powers over questions of trade and economic policy as the U.S. balance of trade with Japan has fallen more and more deeply into deficit. Frustrated over the failure of the domestic economy to strengthen, the United States has grown impatient with what it perceives as Japan's refusal to assume global responsibilities concomitant with its status as a world power; uncertain of the stability of its prosperity and caught in the conflict between its traditional values and those of the West, Japan has grown increasingly resentful of American demands for even more dramatic changes in its way of life.
    It is generally agreed that U.S.-Japanese relations have been marked by heightening tension since the "Nixon Shock" of 1971. But how badly has this tension in the economic sphere frayed the whole system of connections between the two countries? What are the various factors that have contributed to these tensions - what are the sources of American impatience and of Japanese resistance? To what extent can each nation be said to be at fault? Will economic relations deteriorate further, and, if they do, how will this deterioration affect the political, diplomatic, and strategic aspects of our relationship? To what extent might it alter Japan's military posture? What can be done to reverse the process of estrangement and lead both nations out of the

current atmosphere of confrontation back into one of healthy competition and cooperation? Will the situation correct itself as economic forces bring the two nations closer together, or will it be necessary for both Japan and the United States to develop new policies in pursuit of a rapprochement?

In the essays that follow, representatives of the business, financial, academic, and political communities in the United States and Japan address these questions. Their papers grew out of a series of monthly seminars held at the Lehrman Institute from October 1978 to May 1979, which brought together a small group of Japanese and American scholars, businessmen, bankers, and government officials, all concerned with understanding and, if possible, reconciling the economic divisions between the United States and Japan. All the authors recognize that these differences arise in large part from the fact that their respective economies represent divergent - in many ways completely opposing - approaches to the organization of a modern industrial capitalist society.

It is true that the most obvious and immediate cause of the tension between the United States and Japan is the American trade deficit and that economic relations between the two countries would ease if that imbalance were rectified through an increase in American exports to Japan in combination with a decrease in Japanese exports to the United States. However, the trade balance is the result of numerous factors within the economy of each nation, factors which have for their part arisen from historical and cultural processes and which are unlikely to change soon, particularly if no strong impetus for change exists within either society. All of the papers are grounded in the common perception, on both the American and the Japanese side, that the fundamental differences in the economies of our two societies reflect rock-bottom divergences in value systems. As these differences are commonly characterized, the Japanese people save for the future, while Americans tend more to spend their money in the present; Japanese industries are oriented toward increasing their share of the market, while their American counterparts are motivated by the profit principle. American corporations are single entities, treated as individuals under the law and free to act as individuals within certain legal limits; Japanese corporations are social organisms with social responsibilities and are held accountable for their actions by a vast network of individuals and institutions. These and other sets of contrasts grow from one central and fundamental difference in values: the American system cherishes the freedom of individuals to act independently of their fellows, while the Japanese system seeks above all the harmonious coordination of individual wills into a consensus.

This juxtaposition lies at the heart of the economic conflict between Japan and the United States. It is crucial to an understanding of the current difficulties between these two nations because it transcends the purely economic differences between them. Although they share certain goals and values as democratic and capitalist systems, the United States and Japan approach the problems of societal and industrial development from completely opposite directions because of their conflicting perspectives regarding the questions of individual freedom and social harmony. This basic difference gives rise to the contrast in the economies of the two nations between the American bias in favor of the free operation of market forces and the Japanese preference for economic planning and goal setting through the mechanism of consensus. And this difference in values also gives rise to each society's inability to understand the other. The Japanese assert that many American industries are no longer able to compete with their counterparts in Japan and elsewhere because the operation of the free market has not managed to induce investment in new facilities and equipment, and the government has not taken sufficient steps to encourage capital investment, choosing instead to protect these lax industries by limiting competitive imports. Americans, on the other hand, have found solace in the so-called Japan, Inc. myth, which characterizes Japan as a single, tremendously productive corporation, relentlessly churning out exports, both energized and regimented by the spirit of consensus. These are distorted characterizations of the American and Japanese economies, but the distortions are based upon enough truth to give them general currency, and a kind of for-the-sake-of-argument validity. Certainly America's trade deficit, although it may be explained in terms of historical processes, is in large part also a product of the presumably reversible failure of American industry to generate long-term investment. And certainly Japan's economic success is largely the result of the collaboration of several forces which in the United States operate freely, separately, and often chaotically. As Japan's largest market, the United States has been affected by Japan's success more than Japan's other trading partners, and when the peak of Japan's economic triumph coincided with the downturn of the American economy in the early 1970s, Japan became a natural target for American pressure to reduce its surpluses by restraining its exports and increasing its imports.

In response to this American pressure, business and government leaders in Japan feel that they are being used as scapegoats for the failure of American industry to improve its productive capacities. Americans, in turn, argue that Japan's aggressive exporting has engendered hostility throughout the world, that Japan should open its own markets further to world trade, that, in short, the United States is only pressuring Japan to do what it ought to do for its own good.

The Japanese reply that they have already removed most of their barriers to trade and that they cannot impose American demands upon their system without unsettling a precariously balanced government. But the Americans point to the "hidden barriers" to trade that lurk within the inefficient Japanese system for distributing goods and services and argue that the Japanese must accept the responsibilities and risks that accompany their new-found power and prosperity. And so the dispute goes on, producing resentment on both sides because each party believes itself to be pressed into an unfavorable position by the other.

Because this conflict is fueled on both sides by severe domestic difficulties (inflation, unemployment, energy shortages) that show no signs of relenting in the near future, the United States and Japan have reached an impasse in their economic interactions. Several of the essays presented here express little hope for an improvement in relations over the next few years, predicting instead the rise of protectionism in both countries. According to Akira Kojima and Kazuo Nukazawa, whose essays appear below, this shift is likely to be accompanied in Japan by an upswing in nationalism and an endorsement of rearmament, both radical and, to some, alarming, departures from Japanese policy in the postwar era. However, several of the essays see the possibility for the reconstruction of U.S.-Japanese economic relations at some later time. As Masahisa Naitoh indicates, economic forces may themselves bring the two nations into greater equilibrium in the 1980s. In addition, Kenichi Imai points to changes taking place within American and Japanese industry which may encourage greater convergence between the two economies in the future, as American companies become more societal in their orientation, and Japanese industry becomes increasingly shaped by market forces.

The spectrum of opinion which this volume encompasses is, in fact, quite broad, and the differences are not entirely predictable along national lines and areas of expertise. For example, Kiichi Mochizuki, a Japanese industrialist, presents the case for government intervention in the business sector, while Kenichi Imai, an economist, argues for increasing the play of market forces in the Japanese economy. On the American side, Stephen DuBrul depicts Japan as a shrewd and pragmatic survivor, while James Abegglen characterizes Japan's pragmatism as ultimately self-defeating. Despite this diversity, there are numerous points of agreement among the essays. Nearly all of the Japanese authors point to the potential for stagnation and rigidity in the structure of Japan's economy, along with that nation's dependence upon external pressure in order to bring about change. Both sides lament the failure of American leadership, along with the arrogant stance of the United States in its trade negotiations with

Japan. And nearly all the authors stress the need for increasing the exposure of the American public to the problems of Japan and the complexities of the trade issue, since the current swell of protectionist sentiment in the United States is due in part to the manipulation of an uninformed public by the clamor of particular interests hurt by Japan's marketing successes.

It is true that Americans and Japanese know a great deal more today about each other's values, social structures, and economies than ever before. But as several authors point out here, the increasing level of interchange between Japan and the United States is, to a large extent, the product of the trade dispute and is, therefore, a recent phenomenon. Furthermore, this interchange, while it contains a number of noteworthy American contributions to U.S.-Japanese understanding (see, for example, the recent work of Ezra Vogel), still does not adequately represent the perspectives of the Japanese themselves. And this exchange remains wildly unbalanced on the American side: the American public knows much less about life in Japan than the Japanese public knows about life in the United States. A 1979 press survey revealed that the activities of the United States received over ten times as much coverage in the leading Tokyo newspaper as the activities of Japan received over the same period in The New York Times. Whatever its causes, this lopsided interchange has led to the impression among many Japanese that Americans are not interested in them, do not care about them, or, worse, harbor feelings of racial and cultural superiority toward them.

This sense of racial and cultural antagonism continues to underlie much of the economic and social tension between the United States and Japan. On the Japanese side, resentment is often generated by a sense that American officials tend to apply more pressure to the Japanese than they do to their European trading partners, with the activities of the Special Trade Representative singled out in particular. Japanese traders and economists often point to what they regard as hard proof of American prejudice against Japan, namely, the fact that the United States continues to attack Japan on trade matters even though this country has lost more ground to its European competitors (and especially to Germany) in such areas as automobiles, steel, textiles, and electronics than it has to Japan. Americans argue that the United States is not "picking on" Japan, and reject passionately the charge of Occidental racism, but the point is that the impression of Western prejudice persists in Japan, and it frequently surfaced in the deliberations of the seminar group that produced this volume. The misunderstandings that arise from the deep cultural disparity between the United States and Japan inevitably became a recurring theme throughout the course of the seminar meetings, and represent a principal rationale for the publication of these essays. The information gap between Japan and the United States has prevented the formation of intelligent public opinion in each country with respect to the other, and this volume attempts to fill in this gap in order to develop a constituency for rational and well-considered policy on both sides of the Pacific.

The essays begin with a comprehensive review of the patterns of U.S.-Japanese interaction by Masahisa Naitoh of the Japanese Ministry of International Trade and Industry. He argues that the present difficulties between the United States and Japan should be viewed within the context of the entire history of relations between these two countries, a record which has been marked periodically by both congeniality and conflict. Naitoh finds the prospects for future relations somewhat more encouraging, as economic factors help the United States improve its trade position while Japan's growth begins to decelerate and its surpluses to decline. The first group of essays following this overview explores the present atmosphere of confrontation which dominates U.S.-Japanese economic relations. James Abegglen, of the Boston Consulting Group, maintains that Japan has consistently defined its own national interests too narrowly for its own good. According to Abegglen, Japan's restriction of the sphere of its interaction with the rest of the world has made Japan appear selfish and ungenerous and has made other nations all the more hostile with respect to Japan's export behavior. An alternate American view, by Stephen DuBrul, former President of the Export-Import Bank, focuses upon the confused and erratic behavior of American leadership as a source of the difficulties between Japan and the United States. He proposes that Japan's caution and usually successful pragmatism represent a stabilizing force in the relationship and suggests that the possibility of Japan's rearmament and the opening of Chinese markets to Japanese goods may relieve much of the current friction between Japan and the United States. On the Japanese side, Kazuo Nukazawa, Visiting Fellow in Economics at the Rockefeller Foundation, and Akira Kojima, U.S. correspondent for the Japan Economic Journal, turn to the specific issues of the trade dispute, both writers expressing apprehension over the possibility of a "collision" between the two powers. Nukazawa argues that, while both countries are at fault in the trade dispute, the Japanese have relied too heavily upon American pressure to bring about necessary changes in their own economy. Analyzing the political roots of the confrontation over trade, he suggests that, as American leadership becomes more fragmented, Japan will become increasingly hostile to the application of pressure by American trade negotiators. Akira Kojima focuses more upon the historical and societal sources of the trade conflict, noting that a number of misapprehensions on the American side have exacerbated the issue.

Since the confrontation between the United States and Japan is rooted in the fundamental differences between their economies, the next portion of the volume is given over to analyses of the discontinuities between the American and Japanese economic systems. A second essay by Masahisa Naitoh compares the American and Japanese economies sector by sector, and argues that it is primarily the weakness of the industrial sector in the United States that has led to the current deterioration of U.S.-Japanese relations. He characterizes these differences as the inevitable reflections of the opposition between the individualistic value system of the United States and the need for social cohesion in Japan. Benjamin Rowland, of the New York investment firm of Salomon Brothers, argues in turn that the social cohesion remarked by Naitoh as the distinguishing feature of Japanese corporate behavior is becoming increasingly difficult to maintain in the face of Japan's domestic problems. In particular, he notes that the strain of financing the Japanese system of guaranteed lifetime employment is likely to contribute to the breakdown of Japanese self-sufficiency. In the final essay in this section, Kiichi Mochizuki, of Nippon Steel in Houston, contrasts the relationship between the public and private sector in Japan with that in the United States. He assesses the adaptability of both systems to the increase in government intervention which, he argues, will represent the next stage of industrial development.

The closing essays are devoted to the development of policy initiatives aimed at improving the relationship between Japan and the United States. Kenichi Imai, Visiting Professor of Economics at Harvard University, concentrates upon the internal economic system of each nation, and upon the Japanese economy in particular, arguing that, despite their obvious differences, the two economies are tending toward convergence in a number of areas, and that these tendencies should be encouraged through the judicious application of new policies on each side. He is especially concerned with Japan's ability to survive the upheavals it is currently experiencing; he contends that the Japanese must look to the freer operation of market forces in order to adapt their economy to a very uncertain future. Irving Friedman of Citibank, formerly with the International Monetary Fund, turns his focus away from the internal sources of tension and confrontation and toward a consideration of the U.S.-Japanese relationship as a whole. He argues that it is in the national interest of both countries to treat their relationship as an unqualified alliance, and contends that the assorted tribulations of the trade dispute are petty in comparison with the benefits that will flow from the preservation of this now-endangered alliance. Elaborating upon a theme introduced in earlier essays, Friedman regrets the recent predominance of bilateralism in relations between the United States and Japan; he argues that the two powers should usher in a new era of cooperation, not only with each other, but also with the other participants in what is becoming an increasingly interdependent global economy.

The health of that economy obviously depends upon mutual understanding and cooperation among the industrial countries of the world, and the relationship between Japan and the United States represents the major case in point. The problems outlined in the essays that follow are undeniably difficult, but they must not be regarded as being beyond solution. In exploring these issues, the authors point in the direction of their resolution - for example, to the need of the United States to encourage capital investment and rejuvenate its industrial sector, and to the need of Japan to reform its financial and distribution systems, to dismantle its remaining trade barriers, and, in short, to accept its role as a global power. These policy directives are themselves fraught with difficulties, since resistance to them is firmly entrenched in both countries. Nevertheless, the general acceptance of these policy directions throughout the highly divergent essays that follow may be one sign that these two powerful countries will eventually find ways and means of submerging their differences to their own common interest and that of the rest of the world.

Diane Tasca

1 Overview: The Bases for Conflict and Cooperation in U.S.—Japanese Relations

Masahisa Naitoh

Relations between the United States and Japan historically have been marked by alternating periods of cooperation and confrontation, and the present tension between these two nations can be regarded as simply another phase of this historical pattern (see Table 1.1). Internal differences - the clash between the ideologies, value systems, social structures, and national priorities of the two countries - have contributed a great deal to the fluctuations in their relationship over the years. However, the other factors that have significantly influenced the pattern of U.S.-Japanese relations lie largely outside either country, in the changing international environment and in the corresponding shifts in the relative status of the United States and Japan as world powers.

Each country has been characterized throughout its history by an ambivalence regarding its relationship to the rest of the world. In the United States, this conflict can be traced to the split between the universalist idealism of the Founding Fathers on the one hand, and the self-protective isolationism exemplified by the Monroe Doctrine on the other. America's international behavior until the First World War was isolationist and protectionist in nature. Partly as a result of the shift in the balance of power after World War II, America's interaction with the rest of the world underwent a dramatic change, and the universalist idealism of the Founding Fathers became the keystone of American foreign policy. Americans undertook to propagate throughout the world the political, social, and economic principles associated with their ideals of liberty and democracy. This endeavor involved considerable sacrifice on the part of the United States, but one of its most admirable results has been the unprecedented prosperity of the world economy through the operation of the free economic order based on the General Agreement on Trade and Tariffs

Table 1.1. History of U.S.-Japan Relationship

DATE	EVENT	STATE OF RELATIONSHIP
1853	United States Commodore Matthew Perry arrives at Uraga. Japan's period of isolationism ends.	TENSE
1854	A Treaty of Amity is signed with the United States, permitting American vessels to stop at two designated ports.	TENSE
1858	A Treaty of Trade is signed.	FRIENDLY
1868	Meiji Restoration. Emperor Meiji issues an order establishing a new officialdom and proclaiming the direct rule of the Throne in every line of national government.	FRIENDLY
1904	Opposing the advance of Russian influence into Korea, Japan declares war on Russia.	FRIENDLY
1905	The State Senate of California approves the resolution to limit immigrants from Japan.	CONFLICTING
1922	Japan participates in the disarmament conference at Washington.	ALTERNATELY CONFLICTING AND COOPERATING
1931	The Manchurian Incident, resulting in the Japanese domination of Manchuria, breaks out.	ALTERNATELY CONFLICTING AND COOPERATING
1941	Japan launches hostilities against the United States and Britain, thus entering World War II.	CONTENDING
1945	Japan surrenders unconditionally to the Allied Powers on the basis of the Potsdam Declaration. Japanese military forces are demobilized and a program of thorough democratization is instituted. 1945-1951	AT WAR / FRIENDLY AND PROTECTIVE
1951	Japan signs a peace treaty at San Francisco with the United States.	FRIENDLY
1970	Trade negotiations on textiles.	FRIENDLY
1971	Nixon visits China, producing "Nixon Shock."	TENSE YET COOPERATIVE
1973	Oil embargo.	COOPERATIVE
1977	The problems of trade imbalance begin to surface.	TENSE YET COOPERATIVE

(GATT) and the International Monetary Fund (IMF), a system designed and maintained by the United States.

In the 1970s, however, the situation changed. From the Japanese perspective, it looked as if the postwar spirit of internationalism had been eclipsed in America by the reemergence of isolationism in the wake of the decline of American economic, political, and military power throughout the world. This new American isolationism represented an outgrowth of the United States' tragic involvement in the Vietnam War and the emergence of a heightened consciousness of domestic social problems in the 1960s. These developments focused America's attention on its own internal troubles and strengthened the argument of the isolationists that the United States must look to its own house before attempting to solve the problems of the world. Specifically, in the area of trade policy, these trends have favored protectionism at the expense of free trade, an ominous development because it undermines the very basis of the current global economic order.

In Japan too there exists an attitudinal dualism which will have significant consequences for that country's behavior in international affairs. Japan's value system has evolved out of more than one thousand years of isolation and homogeneity. The Western concept of individualism is notably absent from this value system: traditional Japanese ideology is collectivist and strongly isolationist. But Japanese society was permanently changed a century ago, when Japan's curtain of isolationism was lifted. In self-defense, Japan set about acquiring the technology and economic practices of the West, products of a wholly alien cultural context in which individualism and universalism were dominant. Japanese scholars have frequently pointed out that modern Japanese society has been formed by the marriage of Japanese "soul" and Western technique. The strange coexistence of these two elements in modern Japan is observable in the principles of conduct of Japanese corporations, in Japan's distribution system, and in its diplomatic negotiating posture.

Americans tend to believe firmly in the universal validity of their own ideological precepts and hence to regard divergent ideologies as irrational. But from the Japanese perspective, what is, is rational: Japanese society has in fact been fairly successful in adapting what it needs from Western culture to its own particular ideological system. The continuing process of Japan's integration of the social and political precepts of the West into its own ancient culture will be a very long one. In the meantime, it is vitally important that both East and West understand and respect the profound differences between each other's cultures. Because of these differences, the encounter between the United States and Japan can be viewed as no less than a great historical experiment, and it would be tragic if this dialogue developed into a confrontation between renewed American protectionism and traditional Japanese insularity. It is to be hoped that the universalist element in American foreign policy will enable the United States to understand and accept cultural differences in other countries, and that Japan will at the same time succeed in eliminating the irrational parochial strains in its own social value system. Both nations will thereby discover that the values and aspirations they share are ultimately far more significant than those they do not.

One impediment that has grown up in recent years to the U.S.-Japanese dialogue has been the change in the power differential between the two countries. Generally speaking, when there is a very wide difference in power between two countries, and when neither feels in any way threatened by the other (because of different geographic spheres of influence, for example, or differing national aspirations), relations between the two nations will be friendly. However, if the power differential narrows so that the two become competitors, the chances of a more conflicting relationship will increase. U.S.-Japanese relations from the end of World War II until the 1960s exemplify the first situation, and relations prior to World War II, the second.

A similar principle applies to economic relations. Harmony and cooperation will prevail when one of the two countries is clearly dominant, or when the two economic structures are highly complementary. As the economic power relationship becomes more balanced and the weaker country becomes a serious competitor of the stronger, relations will become tense (see Table 1.2). This pattern has clearly proved to be the case in recent U.S.-Japanese economic relations. The "flood" of Japanese exports to the United States has touched off vigorous protests from influential domestic American pressure groups. As a result, efforts by the two governments to adjust their countries' economies to the new situation have increasingly been conditioned by an atmosphere of confrontation. This confrontation, if it persists, threatens to become ever more emotional and to strengthen the revival of protectionist isolationism in the United States. There have been indications that such a trend - with particularly disturbing overtones - has been developing in the United States. In the American press, it is not unusual to find, coupled with complaints about the influx of Japanese imports, statements to the effect that the Japanese have forgotten America's postwar assistance, along with the fact that they are free riders under the umbrella of U.S. military security.

To many Japanese, such sentiments reflect an American superiority complex. More important, this superiority complex is perceived in Japan as a form of Western racism, particularly since Japan is regularly singled out for attacks which America's European competitors are spared. In many ways,

Table 1.2. Major Economic Indicators:
Japan and the United States

	1975	1976	1977	1978
GNP (real) growth				
Japan: 1970 constant price	1.4	6.5	5.4	5.6
US: 1972 constant price	- 1.3	5.9	5.3	4.4
Manufacturing production index				
Japan: 1975=100	100.0	111.2	115.7	123.0
US: 1967=100	116.3	129.5	137.1	145.7
Two-way trade (billions $)				
Japan	113.6	132.0	151.3	176.9
% increase	(-3.4)	(16.2)	(14.6)	(16.9)
US	205.1	238.8	272.5	318.0
% increase	(1.5)	(16.4)	(14.1)	(16.7)
Wholesale price index				
Japan: 1975=100	100.0	105.0	107.0	104.3
US: 1967=100	174.7	183.0	194.2	209.3
Consumer price index				
Japan: 1975=100	100.0	109.3	118.1	122.6
US: 1967=100	161.2	170.5	181.5	195.4
Wage in constant price				
Japan: 1975=100	100.0	103.0	103.4	106.0
US: 1967=100	101.4	102.9	104.1	104.3
Capacity utilization (1975 Japan = 100):				
Japan	100.0	108.3	107.5	110.7
US	73.6	80.2	82.4	84.2
Unemployed persons in 1,000s of persons				
Japan	1,000.0	1,080.0	1,110.0	1,240.0
US	7,830.0	7,288.0	6,855.0	6,047.0
Foreign reserves (millions $)				
Japan	12,815.0	16,604.0	22,848.0	33,019.0
in gold stock	905	-	-	-
US	16,226.0	18,747.0	19,312.0	18,650.0
in gold stock	11,599.0	11,598.0	-	-
Balance on current account (millions $)				
Japan	-682.0	3,680.0	10,918.0	16,534.0
US	18,339.0	4,605.0	-14,092.0	-13,855.0
Trade balance (millions $)				
Japan	-2,110.0	-2,427.0	9,686.0	18,200.0
US	9,047.0	-9,306.0	-30,893.0	-34,187.0

SOURCE: Japan Trade Center

the Japanese market is more open to American products than
the European market is, but it is Japan, and not Europe, that
has been the special target of protectionist attacks in the
United States. It is quite possible that the exploitation of
Japan's image as a protectionist country (an image which,
while once valid, is no longer so today) depends for its
success on the persistence in the West of attitudes of racism
and cultural superiority towards the East.

However, the United States and Japan do not exist in a
bilateral vacuum; both countries must operate within the
international environment, a factor which strongly conditions
the relationship between the two countries. It is widely
observed that the world economy since World War II has been
characterized by the continual multiplication of relationships
and the increasing interpenetration of national economies. The
global role of the American economy has remained very
important, but Western Europe since the late 1950s, and Japan
since the mid-1960s have significantly narrowed their economic
power differential with the United States. Furthermore, since
1973, the oil-producing countries have assumed a major role in
the world economy. This multiplication of the centers of
economic power obviously entails a new recognition of Japan's
economic status and role within the global economic system.
(See Tables 1.3 and 1.4)

The present structure of the world economy consists of
four groups of nations: the developed countries, the
oil-producing countries, the non-oil-producing developing
countries, and the Communist countries. The developed
countries have been turning more and more to protectionism in
the face of pressing economic realities (particularly the large
surpluses accumulated by the oil producers) despite their
efforts on the diplomatic level to foster international economic
cooperation. The non-oil-producing developing countries, for
their part, are suffering an increasing burden of
indebtedness.

From the standpoint of U.S.-Japanese relations, it is
essential to give new order to this complicated multipolar global
economic structure, because constructive bilateral relations
cannot be maintained without a reasonably stable and
harmonious international environment. If both Japan and the
United States are to prosper, the world economy as a whole
must grow steadily. To this end, a system should be created
to channel the surpluses of the oil-producing nations and the
developed countries to aid the developing countries, spurring
their growth and creating new markets. Within such a system,
the International Monetary Fund, the World Bank, and other
financial institutions will have to serve as links between the
developed and oil-producing nations on the one hand, and the
developing nations on the other. A new international monetary
order will be necessary, as well as substantial changes in the

Table 1.3. The Multilateral Character of the World Trade System

World Trade: Exports
(in billions of US dollars, f.a.s.)

Area/Country	1965	1970	1973	1974	1975	1976	1977	1978*
Developed countries	129.7	225.9	411.0	547.9	583.3	647.3	734.8	880.0
USA	27.5	43.2	71.3	98.5	107.6	115.0	121.2	143.7
Canada	8.5	16.7	26.4	34.5	34.1	40.5	43.4	47.9
Japan	8.5	19.3	37.1	55.6	55.8	67.3	81.1	98.4
EEC**	64.8	113.0	212.0	276.9	298.4	328.8	382.0	462.1
France	10.2	18.1	36.7	46.3	53.1	57.2	65.0	79.4
West Germany	17.9	34.2	67.6	89.3	90.2	102.2	118.1	142.3
Italy	7.2	13.2	22.2	30.5	34.8	37.3	45.0	56.1
UK	13.8	19.6	30.7	39.4	44.5	46.7	58.2	71.7
Other developed countries	20.4	33.6	64.1	82.4	87.4	95.7	107.1	128.0
Developing countries	35.2	54.3	106.4	216.8	203.7	248.6	283.3	296.0
OPEC	10.7	17.6	39.6	120.5	111.5	135.3	147.6	145.0
Other	24.5	36.7	66.8	96.3	92.2	113.3	135.7	151.0
Centrally planned economies***	23.2	34.7	61.0	75.5	90.4	99.1	115.8	133.5
USSR	8.2	12.8	21.3	27.4	33.4	37.3	45.2	53.0
Eastern Europe	11.8	18.2	31.7	37.6	45.3	49.5	56.9	64.0
China	2.0	2.1	5.0	6.7	7.2	7.3	7.9	10.0
TOTAL	188.1	314.9	578.4	840.2	877.4	995.0	1133.9	1309.5

*Preliminary.
**Includes Belgium, Luxembourg, Denmark, Ireland, and the Netherlands.
***Includes North Korea, Vietnam, Albania, Cuba, Mongolia, and Yugoslavia.

SOURCE: The 1979 Annual Report of the Council of Economic Advisers (Washington, D.C.: Government Printing Office, January 24, 1979), p. 302.

Table 1.4. The Multilateral Character of the World Trade System

World Trade: Imports
(in billions of US dollars, c.i.f.)

Area/Country	1965	1970	1973	1974	1975	1976	1977	1978*
Developed countries	136.7	235.3	427.2	608.6	610.9	701.5	793.3	912.0
USA	23.2	42.4	73.6	108.0	103.4	129.6	157.6	183.1
Canada	8.7	14.3	24.8	34.4	36.2	40.3	42.1	46.1
Japan	8.2	18.9	38.4	62.1	57.9	64.9	71.3	79.9
EEC**	69.3	116.9	216.4	295.9	301.9	345.6	389.7	462.8
France	10.4	19.1	37.7	52.9	54.0	64.4	70.5	81.8
West Germany	17.6	29.9	54.9	69.6	74.9	88.4	101.5	121.8
Italy	7.4	15.0	27.8	41.1	38.4	43.4	47.6	56.4
UK	16.1	22.0	38.8	55.0	54.2	56.6	64.6	78.6
Other developed countries	27.3	43.0	74.0	108.2	111.5	121.2	132.7	140.0
Developing countries	37.0	56.6	99.4	163.3	189.5	207.2	249.1	291.5
OPEC	6.5	10.0	20.3	33.4	52.7	64.1	87.5	104.3
Other	30.5	46.6	79.1	129.9	136.8	143.1	161.6	187.2
Centrally planned economies***	22.6	34.2	62.0	79.2	100.8	105.1	115.3	133.5
USSR	8.1	11.7	21.0	24.9	37.1	38.2	40.9	49.0
Eastern Europe	11.6	18.5	32.8	42.3	51.3	55.6	61.7	67.7
China	1.8	2.2	5.1	7.4	7.4	6.0	6.9	10.1
TOTAL	196.3	326.1	588.6	851.1	901.1	1013.8	1157.7	1337.0

*Preliminary.
**Includes Belgium, Luxembourg, Denmark, Ireland, and the Netherlands.
***Includes North Korea, Vietnam, Albania, Cuba, Mongolia, and Yugoslavia.

SOURCE: The 1979 Annual Report of the Council of Economic Advisers (Washington, D.C.: Government Printing Office, January 24, 1979), p. 302.

present GATT system for commodity flows. In all these efforts, cooperation between Japan and the United States will be essential.

While it is true that relations between the United States and Japan are currently troubled by friction over economic questions, it is difficult to determine the extent to which these difficulties have altered the overall health of the relationship. Political, economic, and military factors all have a significant bearing upon the current status of U.S.-Japanese relations.

In the United States these days it makes a great deal of political sense to attack Japan. While it may be foolhardy for a politician to propose unpopular solutions to complicated domestic problems, such as rising unemployment, there are few risks involved in blaming those problems upon a foreign country. Understandably, the politics of blame is a popular alternative for those who wish to evade difficult responsibilities. In other words, it is generally more convenient for American politicians to blame Japan for its recent and rapid economic strides than it is to face up to the reality that much of U.S. industry has declined in its international competitiveness. On the other side, it is true that Japan has, upon occasion, been slow to adopt the measures required to improve its economic relations with the West. Major policy change generally comes very slowly in Japan, since a consensus for such change seldom forms quickly. For this reason, foreign pressure has occasionally proved a useful stimulus to progress in Japan; however, this pressure can go too far, provoking the Japanese into intractability. Part of the problem is the apparent Japanese quiescence to criticism on economic and trade matters. When the United States attacks Japan, it expects Japan to respond with the sort of counterattack a Western nation would mount. The Japanese, however, are not accustomed to playing by such rules. The result is the appearance of defensiveness or submissiveness on Japan's part, which makes it all the more convenient as a scapegoat. It is therefore incumbent upon a superpower such as the United States to make a special effort to maintain an attitude of openness and fairness in dealing with its trading partners. With its vast economic resources and military capability, the United States remains by far the world's leading power, and this power can become quite intimidating, even when it is not meant to be so.

Economic issues, of course, have occupied the forefront of the recent difficulties between the United States and Japan. In this connection, it is necessary to keep in mind the fact that there have been many successful cases of American companies investing in and exporting to Japan: examples include Coca-Cola, IBM, McDonald's, and Corning. But unfortunately - and interestingly - these success stories have taken second place to the attention devoted to the failures.

Part of the explanation for this phenomenon lies in the fact that the voices of dissatisfaction and complaint usually prevail over the voices of content. This may be especially true in the United States, a nation of assertive and outspoken people. Certainly Japan receives more criticism from the United States than the actual situation justifies.

A number of reasons can be advanced to explain the extent and intensity of the campaign against Japan on the part of American domestic interests. In many cases, it must be concluded that American business executives criticize Japan largely in order to evade responsibility for their own failings. It is highly significant that, at a time when a number of American products have lost ground in the Japanese market, exports from the European Economic Community (EEC) have actually shown a marked increase. For example, between January and July of 1978, exports from the EEC to Japan rose by 38.7 percent over the same period in 1977, while American exports did not increase at all, despite the appreciation of the yen. This would suggest that the "closed" nature of the Japanese market is not such an impediment to foreign imports as many Americans contend. The significant factor, instead, is the fact that U.S. industry has failed to produce and market its goods competitively.

Japan's critics would argue, on the other hand, that Japanese business practices are excessively competitive. Such complaints about Japanese corporate behavior are inevitable outgrowths of the difference between the Japanese philosophy of business and that of Japan's competitors. For example, the behavior of Japanese companies is based primarily upon long-term considerations, while American firms are more concerned about earning profits in the short run. Japanese firms will actually seek to increase their share of a given market at the expense of profits. At the same time, Japanese companies are extremely quick to grasp consumer needs and to respond to these needs. In Japan, the inventor of a popular product seldom retains the advantage for long, because others soon recognize and rush into a potentially profitable market. Such behavior typifies the extreme competitiveness of Japanese business, which is itself an extension of the competitiveness of a densely populated society.

The economic tensions between the United States and Japan must be interpreted within the context of their respective economic structures. This matter is treated in detail in several of the essays below, but at this point let me simply note that the economic friction between the United States and Japan can be traced in large part to the fact that their economies function in almost completely opposite ways. In Japan, the secondary (industrial) sector of the economy is highly productive and efficient, while the primary (basic material production) and tertiary (delivery system) sectors function very inefficiently. The American economy, on the other hand, is more efficient in the primary and tertiary sectors, and much less so in the secondary sector. Thus Japanese society is much more geared to production than to consumption, while, at present at least, the reverse applies to the United States. Prospective American exporters to Japan either are frustrated by the inefficiency of the Japanese delivery system or find that their basic commodities are blocked by the barriers erected by Japan's inefficient but politically influential primary sector. It should be noted, however, that the outmoded Japanese delivery system does not single out foreign products for discrimination - Japanese industries also must work through this sector, and they too experience frustration in overcoming the obstacles it presents to the flow of goods into the market.(1)   (See Table 1.5 for a breakdown of the U.S.-Japan balance of payments for 1972, 1975, 1976, 1977, and 1978.)

The current state of relations between the United States and Japan can be roughly described as tense yet cooperative, the tension being largely the product of the trade imbalance. In assessing the prospects for U.S.-Japanese relations over the next decade, I would predict that the United States and Japan should be able to overcome their present difficulties in the near future, after which time a more mature "equal partner" relationship will develop between them. This assessment is based on several major considerations:

First, the rapid rate at which Japan has narrowed the economic power gap between itself and the United States will decline. Indeed, in absolute terms, the gap will enlarge (even though Japan will retain an edge in its economic growth rate) because of the much larger size of the American economy. As a result, the United States will be less inclined to view Japan as a bigger economic threat than it actually is.

Second, there is certain to be a reduction in Japan's external surplus as a result of the long-term appreciation of the yen, the implementation of open market policies in Japan, and the intensification of U.S. export efforts. Within five to seven years, the Japanese current account surplus should be reduced by about two-thirds.

Third, a good part of Japan's future export growth will be directed toward other Asian countries - including China - as Japan strengthens its economic ties with these nations. With the diversification of its trade structure and the multiplication of its diplomatic initiatives, Japan can be expected to accept a much more significant role in international affairs. Within this area lies the matter of military policy, a major factor affecting United States-Japanese relations. Japan is and will remain under the American security umbrella, but recent years have seen increasing discussion of the possibility that Japan will raise its level of defense expenditures to three

Table 1.5. The US-Japan Payments Position:
US International Transactions with Japan
(in millions of US dollars)

Items	1972	1975	1976	1977	1978
Exports - goods & services	6,663	12,726	13,572	14,327	18,259
Merchandise, excluding military	4,963	9,567	10,196	10,566	12,960
Travel	205	410	439	450	542
Transportation	516	923	1,008	1,185	1,335
Other services	503	619	676	747	1,026
Receipts of income from assets	476	1,208	1,253	1,379	2,398
Imports - goods & services	-11,427	-14,055	-18,934	-22,362	-29,725
Merchandise, excluding military	-9,076	-11,257	-15,531	-18,565	-24,542
Direct defense expenditures	-839	-764	-794	-822	-950
Travel	-121	-131	-145	-149	-155
Transportation	-425	-727	-1,279	-1,488	-1,615
Other services	-57	-99	-76	-98	-64
Payments of income from assets	-909	-1,078	-1,110	-1,240	-2,398
Unilateral transfers	-42	-43	-43	-43	-73
Balance on merchandise trade	-4,113	-1,690	-5,335	-7,999	-11,582
Balance on goods & services	-4,764	-1,329	-5,362	-8,036	-11,466
Balance on current account	-4,806	-1,372	-5,405	-8,079	-11,538
US assets in Japan, change	-223	1,595	-831	541	-5,995
Japan's assets in US, change	5,087	-548	4,106	6,358	13,749

SOURCE: US Department of Commerce, Survey of Current Business, June 1975, December 1976, 1977, 1978, and June 1979.

times the current level, from 1 percent to 3-4 percent of its
GNP.(2) Japan's increased independence and initiative in
shouldering the responsibilities of a world economic power will
be welcomed by the United States and should enhance Japan's
image in the rest of the world as well.

These premises are grounded in a number of likely
developments over the next ten years in Japan and in the
United States which I would like to trace in some detail here.
Japan's average annual economic growth rate in the 1980s will
be about 6 percent. This contrasts sharply with the 1960s
growth rate of 10.8 percent, which reflected a 9.2 percent
annual rise in productivity and a 1.6 percent annual increase
in the size of the labor force. The projected 1980s growth
rate of 6 percent - which should be regarded as a minimal
requirement for Japan's future economic health - could be
achieved by maintaining a 9.2 percent rate of increase in
productivity with a 3.2 percent decrease each year in the size
of the labor force. Alternatively, if Japan tries to maintain
full employment (that is, an unemployment rate of less than 2
percent) at the 6 percent growth rate, it will have to accept a
productivity increase rate of only about 4.9 percent a year,
with a 1 percent annual increase in the labor force.

This projection of a reduced economic growth rate in
Japan reflects the restraints on growth imposed by resource
limitations. If Japan's share of the world's oil remains
constant, 6 percent appears to be the highest feasible growth
rate for the Japanese economy, even with the maximum possible
use of nuclear energy, liquid natural gas, coal, and other
alternative energy sources.

This low economic growth rate in turn is likely to bring
about a number of significant changes in the Japanese economy
and in Japanese society in the 1980s. Japanese corporate
practices will probably be streamlined considerably (for
example, through reductions in debt/equity ratios), and
corporate activity will be based increasingly upon profitability
rather than upon the market share principle. High profit
industries will tend increasingly to become internationalized.
Sluggish capital investment will ultimately weaken the
international competitiveness of Japanese industry, although
product innovations will continue to be made in response to
consumer tastes, and existing facilities will be modernized to
some extent (without expanding their present capacities).
Unemployment levels will rise, although few changes will be
made in the system of lifetime employment. As one aspect of
the streamlining of corporate practices, wage and salary
increases will be based more upon work performance than upon
seniority. Both of these developments will serve to maintain
the presently strong work ethic of the Japanese labor force.
Little change is anticipated in the behavior of the labor
unions. But the labor force itself will change to some extent

in the 1980s, as Japan will increasingly become an "elderly people's society." The portion of the population over 65 years of age will rise from 8.6 percent today to 11 percent in the 1980s, and over 14 percent by the turn of the century.

As for the American economy, forecasts vary, with American estimates tending to be relatively conservative. For example, Data Resources, Inc. predicts an annual average growth rate of 3.5 percent between 1977 and 1990, with significant deceleration over the course of this period (4.1 percent in 1977-80, 3.6 percent in 1980-85, and 3 percent in 1985-90). However, Japanese research organizations generally project a much higher rate of growth for the American economy. For instance, the Japan Economic Research Center forecasts a 4.1 percent annual growth rate for 1980-85. Inflation is projected to remain close to its present rate over the next four years, after which time it should begin to decelerate. The fixed investment of American business as a share of the gross national product (GNP) should rise from 9.8 percent in 1977 to 11.7 percent in 1990. This prediction is based on an average annual real growth rate of 4.6 percent, as compared with the long-term historic average of 4.3 percent from 1955 to 1973. The U.S. balance of payments is likely to achieve approximate equilibrium throughout the 1980s.

With respect to trade relations between the United States and Japan, the United States will certainly remain Japan's largest export market as well as its greatest source of imports. However, the American share of Japanese exports is likely to decline to about 25 percent in 1985, from 30.7 percent in 1970, while the Japanese share of U.S. exports will increase to about 16 percent in 1985 from 13.6 percent in 1970. Although the volume of total world trade will expand, the Japanese trade surplus with the United States will not rise but will remain in the $5-8 billion range in 1980-85. On the basis of these figures, there is good reason to hope for a judicious solution to the current trade dispute between these two countries over the next few years.

Thus far, the effects of foreign exchange rate adjustments on trade between the United States and Japan have been obscured by differences between the two countries' stages of economic recovery, and by the j-curve effect, among other factors. In the long term, however, the impact of foreign exchange rate adjustments - including their effects on prices - will be felt. It can also be expected that direct Japanese investment in the United States over the next ten years will to some extent substitute for Japanese exports to the United States. On the American side, there is reason to hope that both government and private enterprise will review such fundamental problems as how to stimulate investment and encourage technology research and development (R&D), and how to enhance the export drive of U.S. business through an effective export promotion policy. Positive actions in those areas, combined with a cheaper dollar, offer the prospect of a gradual, but steady and significant, strengthening of the export competitiveness of American industry.

In the coming years, Japan will begin to assume a new, more active and independent role in the arena of international economic cooperation. Especially since the Fukuda Doctrine of August 1977, Japan has sought and will continue to seek closer cooperative relations with the Association of Southeast Asian Nations (Singapore, Malaysia, Thailand, Indonesia, and the Philippines). The ASEAN area is very important to Japan: 80 percent of its imported oil and 40 percent of its total trade in commodities are transported through the Malacca Strait. Moreover, Southeast Asia accounts for 14.5 percent of Japan's imported raw materials, as well as 18.2 percent of its total direct investment abroad. This area is also important in the context of global North-South relations. It is natural that Japan, as the leading economic power in Asia, should assume a primary responsibility for aiding the development of its neighbors to the South. The modernization of the ASEAN countries will take at least ten years; of Vietnam, at least twenty. During this period, these nations will need Japanese economic aid, technology, and markets; clearly, then, continuing cooperation between Japan and the ASEAN group is in the interest of all parties concerned.

The United States does not view Southeast Asia as an area central either economically or militarily to its broad strategic interests. Japan's assumption of responsibility in Southeast Asia, therefore, will most probably be quite welcome to the United States. At the same time, the United States would probably seek safeguards against an overwhelming Japanese penetration of the region: for example, the United States would be likely to prefer that Japanese economic aid to these countries be offered with no strings attached. Some explicit cooperation between Japan and the United States will be necessary in order to enable both countries to determine their appropriate respective roles in the ASEAN area.

As far as the People's Republic of China is concerned, the Sino-Japanese Treaty of August 1978 promises to continue and accelerate the strengthening of relations between these two Asian countries. In my judgment, it will be some thirty years before China has achieved a significant level of modernization, a process in which Japanese cooperation can play a substantial role. Cultural ties between China and Japan can be expected to strengthen as well. In the light of the American recognition of the Peking government, it is reasonable to assume that the United States will continue to lean toward China in the Sino-Soviet dispute, and will therefore regard Sino-Japanese relations as a positive development. In the near future, the United States and Japan will most likely discuss the question of easing Coordinating Committee (COCOM) restrictions against China.

Japan will be expanding its economic relations outside of Asia as well over the next decade. The oil-producing countries will loom larger among Japan's trading partners, as Japan opens its markets and increases its technological aid and other assistance to Saudi Arabia and other nations of the Middle East with a view toward assuring itself of a stable supply of oil from these sources. In order to contribute to the stability of the region, Japan will also extend to Egypt and to the Saudi-oriented nations (Sudan, North Yemen, etc.) offers of economic cooperation and technological assistance. Japan will also steadily strengthen its cooperative relations with Latin America, particularly Mexico and Brazil. In general, these trends in Japanese policy toward greater involvement in the international scene should be much appreciated by the United States and should contribute considerably to the improvement of U.S.-Japanese relations.

It must be understood, however, that Japan's assumption of greater initiative in international economic cooperative efforts will occur only gradually. The pace of change will necessarily be conditioned by Japan's need to develop a national consensus regarding the desirability of playing a more active global role. As noted already, the process of consensus formation is a slow one; moreover, Japanese political leadership as a rule prefers to respond to a new consensus only after it is already formed, rather than attempting to speed its formation.

In conclusion, the chances for stabilizing and strengthening relations between the United States and Japan and for establishing a solid partnership between them in the coming years are excellent as long as both nations can manage to find mutually satisfactory solutions to their present differences. The gravest threat to this prospect is the ascendancy of the protectionist impulse in the United States. Japan too must guard against the impulse to retreat from its responsibilities as a world power. If the American response to domestic pressures should involve a "get tough" policy toward Japan, the result could be a revival of Japan's traditional nationalism and parochialism and a general intensification of mistrust on both sides. America's lax attitude toward the depreciation of the dollar, the Strategic Arms Limitations Treaty (SALT) negotiations, and several phases of the trade negotiations have already created a measure of indignation in Japan, and it is not difficult to discern beneath the surface of Japanese society a resurgence of Japan's age-old impulse toward isolationism. I am hopeful that our two countries will continue to do their very best to understand each other, since mutual understanding remains the best - indeed, the only - guarantee of the close and enduring cooperation which is surely in the interest of them both.

NOTES

1. See James C. Abegglen and Thomas M. Hout, "Facing Up to the Trade Gap with Japan," <u>Foreign Affairs</u>, Fall 1978, pp. 146-168.
2. See Professor Henry S. Rowen, "Japan and the Future Balance in Asia," <u>Orbis</u>, Summer 1977, pp. 191-210, for further discussion.

I

Sources of Confrontation in U.S.—Japanese Relations

2 Narrow Self-Interest: Japan's Ultimate Vulnerability?

James C. Abegglen

When everything is taken into consideration, it may well be the case that Japan's vulnerability as an economy lies in the very nature of its economic success.

It is a commonplace, and an accurate one, that Japan is critically dependent on the rest of the world for the import of the entire range of raw materials and foodstuffs it needs to support its sophisticated and powerful economy. (See Table 2.1 for an analysis of Japan's raw material imports.) Any event that would cut off this external supply would at a single stroke reduce Japan's economy to the level of a century or more ago. Yet it must be clear by now that such external events are unlikely, and moreover, that the various predictions of shortages of materials are becoming increasingly improbable. Even the projections of a shortfall in crude oil supply are being moved steadily forward in time. And the Japanese economy has amply proved its strength and resilience in dealing with inflation, recessions, and exchange rate fluctuations.

Indeed, the Japanese economy is today, despite several years of external and internal difficulties, in robust shape. Inflation is low, the currency is strong, and domestic demand is rising. Mild concern about possible inflation and about continued increases in crude oil prices hardly even ripples the current confidence of both the Japanese business community and the political leadership. It can only be concluded that the strength of the Japanese economic system and the competence of its managers are of a very high order.

It is the burden of this essay that Japan's economic vulnerability in fact lies in Japan's successful maintenance of an internal focus - that, by defining national self-interest in the most narrow terms, and by refusing to undertake initiatives in international policy, Japan is actually risking all

Table 2.1. The Importance of Japan
in World Demand for Raw Materials

Japan's Imports of Selected Commodities, 1975
(in millions of US dollars, c.i.f.)

	Imports from:		Japan's Imports as % of World Imports
	Developing Countries	Total World	
Foods:			
Grain sorghum	123.9	562.7	37.4%
Soybeans	10.4	941.9	22.1
Maize	173.8	1,137.9	14.5
Sugar	1,305.3	1,682.5	12.5
Bananas	163.4	163.4	12.0
Citrus fruit	7.2	121.0	6.4
Nonfoods:			
Timber (logs)	857.1	2,235.6	58.6%
Iron ore		2,197.0	38.0
Coal		3,472.8	34.0
Wool	5.3	477.5	21.3
Crude oil		19,653.3	17.0
Cotton	361.1	827.4	17.0
Tobacco	51.9	288.5	9.9
Rubber	171.5	172.1	9.0

SOURCES: World Bank, Commodity Trade and Price Trends
(1978 Edition), Washington, D.C., August 1978; and
United Nations, Commodity Trade Statistics, 1977.

that its narrow definition of self-interest has so far gained the country.

JAPAN'S INTERNATIONAL ACTIONS

A nation interacts with other nations in only a few dimensions. First of all, it trades with outsiders, an interaction that includes the movement of technology as well as goods across boundaries and currencies. Direct foreign investment represents another interaction, one which is closely related to trade. A nation also provides economic assistance to other countries. Finally, and critically, a nation interacts with others in its defense or military policies. There are other forms of interaction, such as travel and political involvement in addition to that congeries called "cultural interchange," but these are secondary to and derivative of the principal interactions, when they are not downright trivial.

Trade Interaction

Japan's trade interaction with the rest of the world is now a monstrous burden on the world trade system. This burden has fallen most heavily upon Japan's closest trading partner, its critical and still irreplaceable market, the United States. It would seem to be entirely within Japan's self-interest to work actively to help ensure that this market, the American economy, remains strong and vigorous. Yet the lack of clear and visible initiatives in this area conveys the strong impression that Japan will act to redress the trade balance only when the United States presses for such action, and then will act only with the greatest reluctance.

Indeed, even when pressed, Japan's responses are in doubt. At the Bonn Summit, Japan's Prime Minister rashly promised a 7 percent domestic growth rate, a commitment his successor retracted immediately upon taking office. Granted that no leader can in fact promise a given economic growth rate, granted that Mr. Fukuda was perhaps carried away by the splendid occasion at the expense of his better judgment, still, other commitments were offered as well, and they also went unmet. Japan promised to reduce its trade surplus from $10 to $6 billion within the year; in fact, the surplus passed $16 billion. Japan promised an actual deficit on the basic balance of payments; in fact, the surplus is $4 billion.

With respect to trade, the first area of interaction with other nations, Japan is an uncommonly powerful economy, achieving with only brief interruption a large and increasing trade surplus for more than a decade. This surplus was accumulated at a time of considerable difficulty for Japan's principal trading partners, and is a substantial source of damage to the trade positions and currencies of those putative partners. While causing these difficulties, Japan presents itself as a nation that only grudgingly, under the greatest pressure, and with all manner of domestic excuses, makes some modest effort to deal with the problem. Furthermore, even under those external pressures, pledges of policy change seem not to be credible.

Overseas Investment

It might be argued that Japan's trade surplus and accretion of foreign reserves are, in the short run, unavoidable, pending exchange rate shifts and other adjustments - although, of course, these surpluses are not of recent origin, and seem unlikely to melt away. Therefore, Japan's trade partners must look to the second area of international interaction, foreign investment, for some relief.

In this area too, Japan offers little balm either to resource suppliers or to purchasers of its merchandise. Japan's total cumulative foreign direct investment remains small. All the investments ever made abroad by Japan add up to a figure somewhat smaller than the 1978 trade surplus. Nor has foreign direct investment risen rapidly in recent years. Even granting the fact that investment requires lead time, one cannot help but notice that Japan's foreign direct investment has failed to rise above the modest peak it reached in 1973.

The fact that Japanese firms have not invested in the United States in increasing amounts in recent years is the more remarkable in view of the special conditions that have obtained during this period. The yen has strengthened sharply against the dollar, making U.S. assets relatively inexpensive. American share prices have been low, and their purchase has thus been doubly attractive. U.S. economic growth has been higher than normal. At the same time, the savings and investment rate in Japan, and liquidity in general, have remained high. Yet while European companies - particularly German firms - have taken advantage of these very conditions to invest heavily in the United States, Japan, under pressure to help redress the American balance-of-payments deficit, has done little or nothing in this area. Thus, in the second arena of international interaction, Japan also remains internally preoccupied, offering little relief from trade surpluses in the way of direct investment, choosing instead to concentrate its investment in its domestic economy.

Aid and Assistance

What, then, of the third broad area of international interaction, economic aid to less developed countries? Here Japan's record of generosity and initiative is even less impressive than its effort in the areas of trade balances and direct investment. The World Bank reports that Japan's direct development assistance has been maintained for fifteen or more years at about .2 percent of its gross national product. This compares poorly with Germany's direct assistance level of .3 to .4 percent of its GNP, and France's .6 percent. Whatever one might assume about the effectiveness of foreign aid programs, it must be concluded that the free world's second largest economy, running the world's largest trade surplus, and accumulating the world's second largest cache of foreign reserves, has been somewhat less than generous in providing development assistance.

Furthermore, a recent promise to increase aid appears to have been lost in a cloud of niggardly domestic dispute. An undertaking to increase Japanese aid has become the subject of controversy over the appropriate standard to use in measuring that increase. The discussion, rather like the trade discussions, leaves an impression of meanness and reluctance, vitiating whatever advantage Japan might have derived from an expanded aid program. Even more damaging in terms of world opinion is the Japanese policy toward refugees from Vietnam. To date, a grand total of three Vietnamese refugees have been granted permanent residence in Japan. This performance is from a wealthy country, an Asian country, and a country that aspires to the leadership of a peaceful Asia. Whether the opportunity be the munificent one of providing aid, or the humanitarian one of providing refuge, Japan must be seen as acting ungenerously in this area of international interaction as well.

Defense Arrangements

Nothing illustrates Japan's military participation in international affairs better than its attitude toward the recent Soviet moves in the islands immediately to the north of Japan. Only twenty kilometers away from Japan, the Soviets have just established a full airstrip and are reported to be building a missile capability on an island over which Japan - futilely - claims sovereignty. To date, the only observable Japanese response to this move has been the suggestion that Japan might spend as much as 1 percent of its GNP for its military budget by 1983.

The fact is, of course, that Japan is utterly dependent on the United States for its national defense. There is now no significant opposition in Japan to that position, nor is there any substantial support for a program to build an independent capability. Yet it must be evident that the capacity and willingness of the United States to provide Japan's entire defense are becoming increasingly doubtful. Indeed, Japan's trade balance, by its effect on the dollar and its impact on U.S. public opinion, erodes America's ability and willingness to continue to defend Japan. Yet Japan's contribution to the U.S. defense expenditure on its behalf remains modest. The current total contributed by Japan to the maintenance of American forces is some $600 million. When reckoned against the total cost to the United States of its Northeast Asia military establishment and its nuclear umbrella, that offering must be deemed insignificant.

THE JAPANESE EXPLANATION

These are familiar facts. For the most part, Japanese explanations are equally familiar. They are many, and need only be noted briefly here. For example:

- Japan has been isolated for a long while, and internationalization has been thrust on the nation suddenly. A truly international response takes time.
- Japan has special problems with respect to trade, both because of its trade structure with its raw material import dependency, and because of the difficulties of rapidly changing domestic economic patterns.
- Direct investment is often not really justified in terms of competitive costs, and, in any event, Japanese companies have no experience with acquisitions, takeovers, and the other techniques of large and rapid foreign investment.
- Aid programs, to be effective, require careful planning by both donor and recipient, and, to cite one example, the ASEAN countries have not provided proper conditions for massive development assistance. With respect to refugees, Japan is a small and homogeneous country into which refugees cannot be introduced without great difficulty.
- Japan's war experiences, and the resultant public antipathy to the military, make substantial defense expenditure politically impossible. Furthermore, an immediate threat from the Soviets or any other quarter seems unlikely.

These and the many other explanations offered by Japanese apologists are all valid. Each of Japan's policies does indeed have a basis for justification. Indeed, much time is devoted by non-Japanese to advancing these arguments. However, the real issue is not a question of any single behavior or policy. Rather, the issue is the totality of these behaviors and the image of Japan which they present to the world.

While friendly observers can reasonably offer these justifications for Japanese policy, it is also reasonable to regard each of these arguments as simply self-serving, as a rationale advanced by a nation that defines its self-interest narrowly and takes selfish advantage whenever and wherever it can. All of Japan's interactions with the rest of the world in trade, investment, aid, and defense can be interpreted as those of a country acting purely in self-interest, with regard only to consequences for itself. Japan seems to change its international policies only in response to threats, and thus appears to the rest of the world to act in a defensive and ungenerous manner. It is this perception of Japan, and the reactions and interactions that flow from this perception, that may well prove to be Japan's ultimate vulnerability.

THE DEFINITION OF SELF-INTEREST

Assume for the moment a Japanese commentator on these remarks, one of a rather cynical frame of mind. Such a commentator might well offer the view that all nations should and, in fact, do act in their own self-interest. He or she might argue that the world would be much better served if more nations defined self-interest with the precision that Japan appears to have used. Indeed, such a Japanese commentator would gain a sympathetic and supportive audience among many Americans who feel that their nation too might be better served by a narrower definition of self-interest. What, after all, does it matter what others think of Japan?

The fact that nations, like individuals, act according to their own self-interest, and that, indeed, they should do so, is clear enough. But in the case of Japan's apparent policies, two questions arise. First, is Japan really acting in its own interest, especially with respect to trade? And second - and far more important - is Japan defining its self-interest so narrowly as in fact to jeopardize its own well-being?

Narrow Self-Interest

Japan's trade surpluses, especially since they are not deployed in investment or aid, must be viewed as a tax on the Japanese public. Materials are purchased from abroad, and value is added in capital, labor, and technology in Japan to produce goods. These goods can then be consumed. However, in Japan's case, some surplus of goods is needed for sale abroad in order that more materials can be purchased. The problem arises when more goods are produced and sold abroad than are necessary for Japan's purchase of materials. The fact that Japan has accumulated a trade surplus means that goods are sold abroad rather than consumed in Japan, in exchange for currencies that, given Japan's other policies, are not put to use. This imposes on the Japanese public a lower standard of living than their high level of productivity might otherwise attain. In this sense, the U.S. deficit serves self-interest better than the Japanese surplus does. The world provides the United States with goods of real value which are paid for with a depreciating currency and with borrowings. A still more cynical observer might conclude that the American public does better on the exchange than the Japanese public does.

The tax on the Japanese public can be illustrated very plainly. Take the example of food, surely the most basic of family needs. As it happens, the Japanese family eats about 45 percent less food than the American family - 509 kilograms as compared with 758 kilograms. At the same time, the food expenditure per family is 15 percent higher in Japan than in the United States: the American family spends less than one-fifth of its income on food, while the Japanese family spends one-third of its income on food. Japan's level of direct taxation is relatively low. Yet in the case of food, a massive hidden tax is being imposed on the Japanese family as a result of the unwillingness of the Japanese government to make foodstuffs readily available from the world market. Japanese rice prices are four times world levels, wheat prices three to four times, and for such less basic items as beef, the multiple can only be guessed.

Trade restrictions impose many such taxes on the Japanese public. International telephone call charges and air fares are held at very high levels. The entry of new pharmaceuticals to the market is delayed. The fact is that, even according to a narrow definition of self-interest, it would appear that Japan's trade policies are actually hurtful: far from benefiting from these policies, the Japanese people are often penalized by them.

Japan's Real Self-Interest

The more important aspect of Japan's policies, however, is their second order effect. It must be evident that Japan is the most interdependent of the world's major economies. That is, Japan is least able to maintain itself separately from other nations. Japan is dependent on the increasing supply of materials, foodstuffs, and fuels, with no prospect other than that of heightening this dependency. Therefore, it is in Japan's interest to encourage investment in resource development abroad as well as a steady flow of supplies from those investments. More than any other developed nation, Japan needs a world monetary system and a healthy world trade system to insure its continued access to the materials it lacks. And above all, Japan requires either an American defense apparatus to protect itself, or a world order so benign as to make defense systems unnecessary.

Thus, it is in Japan's purest self-interest to actively promote the health of its major markets in North America and Europe, and especially the United States. Those markets provide the funds that enable Japan to purchase materials. Damaging those irreplaceable markets in the short run damages Japan in the long run.

The case of investment is similar. It is entirely in Japan's own interest to invest heavily on a global scale in the development of new resources to insure Japan's supply of raw materials. Their full availability assures Japan of reasonable prices, and the flow of funds and materials supports the trade system upon which Japan ultimately depends. Finally, the health of the American economy in the world system determines whether Japan has a defense capability or not.

The point need not be belabored. It is evident that narrow self-interest, as manifested by massive trade surpluses and niggardly investment and aid programs, in fact works against Japan's real national interest. Japan has prospered during, and in good part because of, a lengthy post-World War II period of relative peace, world economic growth, and international trade. Japan's continued prosperity depends upon the continuation of those trends. Japan can hardly withdraw at this point to a narrow band of Asia; its economy and its needs have outstripped regional solutions, and require that the world be receptive to, supportive of, and interactive with Japan.

THE QUESTION OF IMAGE

The problem of Japan's image is neither remote nor abstract; it finds expression in the current behavior of other nations towards Japan. Japan is seen as narrowly self-interested, and the responses of other countries to that perception are becoming overtly hostile. Images do matter. They are not merely the products of advertising or public relations campaigns, and they do not yield to the mere cosmetics of media treatment. Images are formed out of facts, and they shape responses and decisions.

For example, it appears to be the case that in general the United States is perceived as a well-meaning - if frequently wrong-headed - country. The image of benevolence was formed out of many things, some as tangible as the Marshall Plan, some as slight as the Peace Corps. Still, the general image of the United States has allowed this nation to make the most dreadful errors in policy and be on occasion egregiously self-serving, and still retain some stock of good will on which to draw in need. This image has been, after all, not inappropriate, and, while it may be changing, it still has real value.

In contrast, the rest of the world does not perceive Japan as being generous or well-meaning, and that perception matters. For example, the Japanese government recently engaged an American research organization to examine non-tariff trade barriers in order to advise on those that might be lifted. Even if we leave aside the oddness of commissioning a foreign group to make such a study, the exercise seems to miss the point of present reality entirely. Japanese trade barriers of all kinds have been removed steadily and rapidly over the past fifteen years. They are no longer more substantial than those of other advanced countries. Yet the magnitude of hostility toward Japan with respect to trade matters has risen rapidly during that same period. Indeed, there seems to have been a rather neat inverse relationship. It can be argued that the issue is not a particular trade barrier or two, nor one particular government policy or another. The issue is rather the generally held view that Japan is an ungenerous and narrowly self-seeking participant in world affairs. If general good will toward Japan prevailed, it seems unlikely that hostile feelings about trade would have reached their present pitch; instead, Japan's trade behavior would have been regarded as temporarily aberrant, and would have been tolerated accordingly. But given the actual existence of a strongly negative view of Japan throughout the world, hostile feeling may well find even further expression.

Image matters. And image is built in large part from substance. Japan's image in the world includes many components that are unfavorable, and no amount of friendly publicity will remove them as long as they are based on fact. In most of its interactions with the rest of the world, Japan does in fact act according to narrow self-interest. Of course, it has its reasons, but these reasons do not alter the facts. Continued pursuit of narrow self-interest, without changes in policy and practice, will in fact damage Japan. The damage is unlikely to be restricted to the area of trade discussion. Global hostility toward Japan manifests itself over trade issues because the problems with Japan are currently most acute in this area. But the more critical issues of resource allocation and defense policies will eventually become sources of friction

if Japan's current preoccupation with narrow and parochial
concerns continues.

The challenge to Japan is evident and enormous. Quite
drastic changes are called for in trade policy, in investment
policy, and in aid policy. Japan urgently needs to change its
pattern of interaction with the world, since the consequences
of Japan's past and present self-centered behavior are being
felt. The question is whether Japan can alter its traditional
role in world affairs rapidly enough and drastically enough to
meet its own needs. The passive, receptive role Japan still
plays in the international arena is now obsolete, and the
burden of change rests with Japan.

3 Japanese Autonomy and American Vulnerability: Another View of U.S.— Japanese Relations
Stephen M. DuBrul

There is a striking contrast between the posture of the U.S. trade negotiators and Congress toward Japan and the attitude of the American business community towards its Japanese counterpart. While government officials preach at Japan and Congress rattles its trade sword, American business leaders, who engage in daily commercial combat with Japanese industry, are too impressed with the successes of their Japanese adversaries to presume to tell them what to do. This respect and admiration - albeit tinged with envy - represent a healthy development in U.S. - Japanese relations, and one which may eventually prevail in the official bilateral discussions between these two countries. However, the immediate future holds out little promise of any such change in U.S. behavior towards Japan: at the official level, the United States will continue to moralize and threaten Japan with the specter of a protectionist Congress, while Japan will continue to struggle to accommodate itself, courteously but with increasing resentment, to American demands.

Because of its bullying attitude, the United States must accept a large share of the blame for the current tension in political and economic relations between itself and Japan. But these difficulties are only partially the result of the trade dispute that has preempted our bilateral discussions for some time now. Other factors strain the relationship between the United States and Japan, and the fact that they are pushed aside in the concern over the trade imbalance only adds to the tension channeled into the direct confrontation over trade. The United States and Japan should face these questions squarely, for they underlie our past conflict as well as our present difficulties over trade, and they also speak to the issues that should be of greatest concern to both nations during the last decades of this century. Let me very briefly

32

touch upon what I regard as the most significant among these
"other problems" in U.S. - Japanese relations.

First and above all are the questions of race and culture.
Japan has the most linguistically and ethnically homogeneous
population of any major power in the free world, and the most
literate one as well.   The contrast between America's high
degree of racial, cultural, and educational differentiation and
Japan's homogeneity explains much of the present tension
between the two countries.   Neither can fully appreciate the
other's social problems and priorities because the two societies
are constituted so differently.   This attribute of U.S. -
Japanese relations is so obvious that it nearly goes without
saying, but the implicit acceptance of the fundamental
differences between the Japanese and the American people has
led us to ignore or forget the tremendous impact of these
differences upon every aspect of our interaction.   For
example, the fact that the Japanese labor force contains a vast
number of highly skilled and motivated workers will continue to
give Japan an international economic edge for the remainder of
this century, at least, and one which will not be offset by any
number of currency adjustments or trade concessions.

Even more important, the cultural barrier between the two
nations is compounded by the Japanese perception of Occidental racism.   Many Americans insist that this sensitivity is
unfounded, or worse, they refuse to acknowledge it altogether.
Nevertheless, the belief that Westerners harbor a prejudice
against the Japanese is widespread in Japan, and, if only for
this reason, it represents a significant barrier to full
understanding between the United States and Japan.
Furthermore, this belief is by no means unfounded.   The
Occidental prejudice against the Oriental has been
demonstrated a number of times in the last hundred years: in
the Oriental Exclusion Acts of the nineteenth century, in the
League of Nations debates in the 1920s, in the Congressional
debates over Oriental immigration, and above all, in the
economic and cultural rape of Japanese-Americans during World
War II.   In a sense, it continues to be manifested in the fact
that periodic summit meetings involving the "Group of Seven"
include only one Oriental: Japan is obviously carrying the
economic baggage for all of Asia.   The Japanese feel, perhaps
rightly, that their full membership in the exclusive set of
wealthy nations is checked and qualified by Western racism,
and that they are therefore not treated as equals by their
Western partners.   This suspicion leads the Japanese to
perceive Western demands upon their country as
condescending, inequitable, and even unreasonable, and thus
relations between the United States and Japan are complicated
by emotional factors that do not enter into America's disputes
with its other allies.

The current mold of U.S. - Japanese relations was cast
early in the postwar era. The United States, enjoying the
superior position as military victor, could afford to be generous and indulgent to its recently defeated adversary so long
as Japan humored its benefactor by taking on the role of the
humble penitent. (To some extent, the present-day power
elite in Japan represents a generation that still perceives
Japan's weaknesses as far outweighing its strengths, a fear
that leads to no small degree of concern that the West is
"picking on" Japan.) The difficulty is, of course, that while
Japan has outgrown the role of the humble penitent, and while
the United States has lost the confidence that buoyed its
postwar largesse, the old patterns of behavior have persisted.
The United States still assumes that it has the right to dictate
to Japan, and Japan to some extent still accepts that claim,
but each nation resents the role it must play in relation to the
other. Japan chafes under the burden of its indebtedness to
the United States, while the United States accuses Japan of
ingratitude and irresponsibility in its dealings with its
benefactor and, indeed, with the rest of the world as well.
The United States and Japan, in other words, persist in an
outmoded psychological relationship which calls to mind
analogies of teacher and student or of parent and child, and
which is rendered all the more sensitive by the racial and
cultural differences between the parties involved.

It must also be kept in mind that the United States is not
wholly in the wrong. The Japanese are every bit as proud
and parochial as the American people are. The leaders of the
Japanese government and business community have as yet not
given the United States reason to believe that Japan will
voluntarily assume the burden of economic leadership
commensurate with its present-day economic power. This
perception of Japan's reluctance to relinquish the aggressive
economic practices of a developing economy has fed the
American sense of moral imperative over Japan, as well as
Japan's own sense of moral obligation toward the United States.

America's attitude of moral superiority to Japan is, of
course, also nurtured by the fact that the Japanese receive
"free" military protection from the United States. However,
the apparent decline of American power in the last decade,
coupled with the apparent constriction of America's sphere of
interest, has led the Japanese into concern about the
trustworthinesss of the United States as an ally and trading
partner. For in the 1970s, the racial and historical sources of
dissonance in U.S. - Japanese relations have been amplified by
what must be regarded as the unreliable and irresponsible
behavior of the United States on the international scene. In
the area of the economy, Washington has not sustained a
coherent international policy at any time during this century,
and the existence of such a vacuum grows more and more dan-

gerous as the world economy grows increasingly interdependent. As recently as 1976, there were no fewer than fifty-five committees, agencies, and bureaus in the executive and legislative branches charged with directing various aspects of international economic policy. And since there is no reason to anticipate any significant change in this situation in the near future, Japan, along with America's other industrial partners, will simply have to continue to bob and weave in response to this country's unpredictable and embarrassing policy flailings.

Indeed, apart from the Organization of Petroleum Exporting Countries (OPEC) price increases since 1973, most of the postwar jolts to the Japanese system have originated in Washington. Certainly the unwinding of America's involvement in Vietnam and this country's subsequent withdrawal from Southeast Asia shocked the Japanese people and weakened America's credibility as an authority figure. The greater shock for Japan, however, was President Nixon's dramatic and secretly planned trip to Peking in 1972. Since 1945, U.S. strategic relations in Asia had been conducted almost exclusively through Japan, with Japan in turn providing forward bases for the American military presence in the northwest Pacific. An elaborate strategic interdependence was constructed between Japan and the United States in the 1950s and 1960s, as evidenced by the terms of the Security Treaty of 1960. Nixon's unilateral China initiative in 1972 shattered this structure altogether, as the President played his "China card" and then informed Japan only after the fact. This one incident alone would have provided Japan with ample cause to doubt America's reliability as an ally, but the Japanese received further proof of the capriciousness of American foreign policy in 1978, when President Carter announced the termination of the Security Treaty between the United States and Taiwan in order to establish diplomatic relations with the People's Republic of China. The Japanese could not fail to note the fact that the language of their own security treaty with the United States, like that of the Taiwan treaty, requires only one year's notice of termination. This is not to say that the United States is likely to abrogate its relationship with Japan as abruptly as it did the one with Taiwan, but the point is that the United States has in recent years been behaving increasingly erratically on the international scene and has thereby shaken its nearest allies profoundly. And since, of all its allies, Japan may be counted as the most dependent upon the continuing strength and stability of the United States, America's own capricious international behavior must be regarded as a significant contributor to Japan's growing reluctance to respond to American demands in matters of trade and economic affairs.

Paradoxically, Japan's increasing independence from the United States may be one of the most promising aspects of the relationship. Such independence might enable Japan to free itself from its burden of inferiority - real or imagined - to the United States, and it may also free the United States from its current readiness to play upon Japan's sense of indebtedness. The principal signals of a more equitable, mature relationship between Japan and the United States all grow from what appears to be Japan's development of a stronger sense of an independent national identity. Indeed, for all its protestations over U.S. foreign policy "shocks," Japan has been developing the ability to weather these jolts and set an independent course of its own. For example, after Nixon announced his China move in 1972, Japan did not wait for the inevitable American recognition of Peking before taking action of its own. Instead, Japan seized the initiative in 1972 to return to the Asian mainland peacefully, for the first time in this century; promptly severing its diplomatic - but not its commercial - ties with Taiwan, Japan returned to an ancient stalking ground to reopen a familiar export market for its next generation of hardworking children.

For Japan, the connection with China may prove to be the primary stabilizing force throughout its economic readjustments over the next few years, and it is clearly within the interests of the United States to encourage Japan's already aggressive China initiative. The enormous capital and human needs in China are virtually tailored to Japan's capabilities, and, instead of exporting its employment problems to the United States, Japan may be able to export them to China, on mutually beneficial terms.

In sum, as the economic dream of postwar Japan has moved toward reality, the country has grown relatively immune to the periodic seizures of American foreign and trade policy. In turn, this healthy immunity has enabled Japan to follow an increasingly independent and muscular economic course of its own. The opening of China at this particular time may prove to be an important emotional and economic advance for the relationship between Japan and the United States.

Today, Japan stands as the economic giant of Asia. It has made and continues to make strategic investments in resources and markets throughout the free world. It has embarked on a massive program of cooperation with China. It continues to flirt with the Soviet Union over the possibility of exploring Siberian and offshore mineral resources. In short, Japan possesses all the economic credentials it needs to play with the other major powers. It lacks, however, the military credentials to play the game effectively.

Japan's defense is completely dependent upon American naval and air power and upon American good will. Yet the U.S. military presence throughout Asia is being steadily reduced, while the Soviet presence is being dramatically enhanced on land, on sea, and in the air. The establishment of Russian bases on the horn of Africa and in Vietnam would place the Soviets directly on Japan's lifeline to Europe and the Middle East; in such a situation, the U.S. Seventh Fleet would be of dubious value. And with American foreign and defense policies in the hands of officials who by and large have had no more than a modicum of international experience, Japan must be increasingly concerned over the prospect of its own strategic defense. To continue to depend upon the good offices of the United States would be sheer folly on Japan's part.(1)

Aside from the visibly growing Soviet threat, there are other factors that suggest that Japan's rearmament must take place soon. First and foremost is the "China Connection" and the 1978 treaty with the People's Republic. The Chinese, anxious over the Soviet military buildup both to the north and to the south, have actively encouraged Japan to become the armory of the Orient. And within Japan itself, a number of domestic forces have been pushing for a reopening of the whole question of defense. The unions, despite a pacifist bias, can recognize the economic implications of idle shipyards, steel mills, and heavy equipment plants, and, what is more to the point, the political implications of idle labor. Japan's present-ly unused facilities could be staffed with workers to rebuild a navy, roll armor plate, and build new tanks. Already business and government have indicated that they want a share in the manufacture of military aircraft, specifically the F-15 and P-3C. Of course, the economic impact of Japan's rearmament will be dwarfed by its geopolitical significance. However, it is clear that rearmament could facilitate some sectoral restruc-turing in Japan, and, in addition, the manufacture of current weapons systems has a seductive appeal to economic planners seeking commercial leverage in any government program.

I believe that Japan will surpass Germany, and possibly even China, in defense spending by 1983. This would rank Japan directly after the Soviet Union and the United States in military expenditures. By the mid-1980s, Japan could have a strategic naval and air capability, thereby beginning to fill the void left by regressive U.S. military policies.(2)

Today Japan has become one of the handful of economic heavyweights in the world. It has achieved this status in less than a generation, through a combination of unbelievable ag-gressiveness, unusual skill, and undaunted determination. Now that Japan has become a major power, it must be accorded the treatment due to a major power, but it must also earn this treatment by assuming the responsibilities appropriate to its position. In short, Japan will need to channel or redirect some of the remarkable energies that have brought it so far so fast. Two events may enable Japan to reallocate its national energies: the opening of China and the rearmament of Japan as an independent military power. These events may also bode

well for relations between the United States and Japan by removing a major source of friction from between the two nations
and by forcing both countries to reformulate their alliance in
terms that reflect the true strengths and weaknesses of both
sides.

NOTES

(1)   See Bernard K. Gordon, "Japan, The United States and
      Southeast Asia," Foreign Affairs, April 1978, pp. 579-
      600.
(2)   See Larry A. Niksch, "U.S. Troop Withdrawal from South
      Korea," The U.S. Role in a Changing World Political
      Economy: Major Issues for the 96th Congress (Washing-
      ton, D.C.: Government Printing Office, 1979), pp. 403-
      423

4 The U.S.—Japanese Collision Course

Kazuo Nukazawa

The two giant economies of the United States and Japan may be heading for a collision over trade in the near future, a collision which will result in substantial damage to the United States and even more serious injury to Japan. In addition, adverse impact will be felt elsewhere throughout the world - in Latin America, Africa, Oceania, and, most particularly, in Asia. And even if a crisis can be averted this time around, the threat of a U.S.-Japanese collision will not diminish until the substructure of misinformation, mistrust, and inertia that underlies the recurrent confrontations between our two countries is dismantled.

Throughout the 1960s and early 1970s, Japanese trade officials relied heavily upon the authority of the Organization for Economic Co-operation and Development (OECD), GATT, and IMF to liberalize Japan's trade and foreign investment policies. Japanese negotiators communicated the impressions they gained at meetings with their Western counterparts as Delphic utterances, to compel the unquestioning cooperation of their fellow citizens. In the process, only the academics emphasized the essential advantage of giving wider access to foreign imports and capital in Japan. Japanese business leaders and government officials chose for their part to focus instead on the logic of external threat: "We have to give them a bit of a concession," such leaders would argue, "or else they will close their markets to us." This mode of persuasion was relatively successful in the 1960s, when "they" referred to the international community; to the extent that the threat was general, it was anonymous. But, since the late 1960s, the United States has singled itself out of the crowd by preferring to use the bilateral setting for negotiating trade disputes.(1) This preference makes a certain amount of sense from the American point of view: the bilateral setting is more effective,

at least in the short run, and American negotiators - always
novices in Geneva and transient sojourners in Washington - do
not favor time-consuming international procedures. But as a
result of the American emphasis upon bilateralism, the economic
dispute between the United States and Japan has become the
focus of Japan's international economic policy, and the United
States has taken upon itself the thankless and unpopular role
of browbeating Japan into the liberalization of its trade
posture.

Japan has become dependent upon this external pressure
because it has failed to develop a sufficiently strong internal
commitment to the promotion of free trade. As has been the
case with economic and technological development, Japan's
trade liberalization was fueled by its postwar zeal to catch up
with the West and become a member of the society of wealthy
nations. Indeed, trade and capital liberalization served as a
kind of initiation fee into the GATT-IMF-OECD club. As noted
above, Japanese officials tacitly agreed to emphasize the
serious threat of possible foreign sanctions against Japan "if
we are seen dragging our feet." The typical line of
persuasion was: "The international lack of understanding of
Japan's unique background is deplorable. But they outnumber
us. Therefore, while we make more efforts to gain their
understanding of our social and economic system, we must
accommodate their demands." Perhaps many of these leaders,
having lived in the West at various times during their
education and careers, were themselves truly committed to the
principle of free trade. However, they never presented the
argument for Japan's liberalization as a question of conviction
but rather interpreted it as a matter of international
head-counting. In any event, very few of them seemed to be
aware of the fact that the further democratization of Japanese
society depended upon the further liberalization of the
Japanese economy. The result was obvious: although Japan's
various concessions to foreign demands for liberalization were
implemented quite smoothly (the advantage of an impassive
bureaucratic system), the liberalization process itself lost all
momentum whenever pressure failed to come from abroad.

This situation became particularly unfortunate for Japan's
economic policies when Asian nations which were not members
of the industrialist club began knocking on Japan's door;
Japan needed very badly to develop a trade posture based
upon something other than its eagerness to compete on equal
terms with the West. When the European Economic Community
turned inward and the less developed countries opted to press
for an institutionalized, rather than market-led, shift of
resources to the Third World, Japanese policy makers
recognized Japan's need to strengthen its ties with its
somewhat neglected Asian neighbors. These officials relied
partially upon the traditional Japanese romanticism towards

Asia, a sentiment very much akin to the guilt complex which first-generation Tokyoites feel toward the pastoral rural areas where the tombs of their ancestors lie. This odd sense of responsibility has been bolstered by Japan's increasing insecurity over America's withdrawal from the Pacific and Russia's bear-hugging of Vietnam. This uneasiness has created a real impetus in Japan to provide economic support to the free nations of Asia in the form of trade concessions, investment, and foreign aid. Japan has also tried, abortively, to keep Vietnam reasonably interested in straddling the fence between the Socialist bloc and the free world. But despite these genuine Asian concerns, it will be some time before ASEAN or any single country in the area (for example, China or Korea) takes over the American role of spurring the efforts of Japanese trade officials to open Japan's market. And Japan's recent attempt to establish "special relations" with such trading partners as Australia and Brazil serves as just one more instance in which trade liberalization is regarded by the Japanese as a concession to persistent outsiders rather than being viewed as it must be, as a national economic policy choice.

Because of this absence of an overall guiding principle in the area of international economic policy, trade policy makers in Japan face two very significant difficulties at this time. First of all, Japan's trade posture has by now been liberalized to the point that only hard-core agricultural items remain under the current residual import restriction system. The elimination of any one of these twenty-seven items would certainly cost the Liberal Democratic Party (LDP) seats in the Diet, where it can no longer be certain of its control of the committee deliberations. The LDP's political base is agrarian, and if the party loses seats through its removal of agricultural import restrictions, it is quite likely that a government with a populist and nationalist tilt would be formed, a government, needless to say, more prone to protectionism. Thus it is becoming increasingly difficult for the present government to justify any further liberalization of Japan's trade policies. The protection of agricultural commodities is deeply entrenched in Japan; even free-trade-oriented academics advocate the continuation of agricultural import restrictions.

The second major problem for Japan's trade policy makers is the fact that concern has been mounting in Japan over both economic and military security after the "oil shock" and recent American withdrawals from Asia. While the traditional Japanese "hunger mentality" is now dying, the anxiety over security is fast replacing it. It is important to remember that the image of war in Japan is repugnant: where war may be a question of honor and justice for many Americans, for the Japanese, who spent years during World War II eating blades of grass, it is more a matter of hunger and misery. But although the prospect of rearmament disturbs many Japanese, the prospect of Japan's defenselessness is perhaps even more frightening. Like the agricultural issue, the security issue stimulates emotional nationalism, an attitude that renders Japan much less tractable at the negotiating table. Thus both Japan's feeling that it cannot make any more trade concessions without jeopardizing the government and its increasing sense that it might not be able to rely upon the United States to guarantee its security are likely to maintain and even heighten the level of economic tension between Japan and the United States.

Of course, the economic dispute is two-sided, and the United States has without doubt contributed its share of the tension, largely as the result of numerous factors on its own domestic front. The American system of government is - whether for good or ill - more democratic than the Japanese system: the legislative branch wields more power in the United States than in Japan, and party loyalty is much weaker when it comes down to specific issues. In the United States, the time-honored Congressional seniority system appears to be giving way to the "juniority" system; leadership has been fragmented, and voting decisions on the Hill are increasingly influenced by "single-issue" politics. American legislators need to maintain their grass-roots support if they are to survive politically, and it happens that trade policy has traditionally been a prime grass-roots issue, involving as it does labor-intensive product areas that represent large voting blocs. American protectionists tend to emotionalize and simplify trade issues, so that the protectionist argument can be accepted by the widest possible stratum of the voting public. In contrast, the Emergency Committee for American Trade (ECAT), representing the advocates of free trade, has addressed its campaign largely to the more sophisticated Washington audience and to the mass media, but it has not appealed to those sectors of the electorate which make or break most American politicians.

One of the most primitive tactics for emotionalizing the trade issue is to establish the image of your adversary's "unfairness": hence American protectionists often use the argument that Japanese exporters are subsidized by the government, and that competition with Japanese manufacturers is therefore unfair. The danger of such an emotional argument is that the bad image survives the measures taken to correct it. For example, even after the bilateral textile issue was resolved by the Multi-Fibre Agreement, the impression has remained among Americans that Japanese industry is subsidized, that its tariffs are higher than those of the United States, that its wages are lower, that American textile exports to Japan are restricted, etc. The actual facts of the matter tell a different story: the average textile tariff level is 23 percent for the United States and 11 percent for Japan; the

industry's hourly wage in the United States is $5.63, while in
Japan it is $5.35. Textile imports into Japan are not
restricted, and the subsidy, where it existed, has been more
than neutralized by the various exchange rate changes over
the last eight years. And even though American allegations
regarding Japan's superior competitiveness have become more
sophisticated recently, focusing upon Japan's industrial
structure, system of financing, administrative guidance,
distribution, and lifetime employment, they are still
nevertheless accompanied by an emotional and moralistic
undertone.

    In the face of the grass-roots emotionalism generated by
the protectionists, the United States Congress has actually
shown rather remarkable legislative restraint thus far, but the
Congress has indicated to the Carter Administration as well as
to foreign governments that this restraint may not last much
longer.(2) The U.S. trade negotiators have found the threat
of protectionist legislation a convenient tool for prying
concessions from trading partners. The Office of the Special
Trade Representative (STR) has in fact been quite successful
in manipulating Congress on the one hand and America's
trading partners on the other. Supreme within the narrow
confines of trade policy, segregated from overall diplomatic
considerations, the STR enjoys hegemony over the State
Department, and boasts excellent liaisons with both the
Congress and the President. During the process of utilizing
Congressional pressure to wrest concessions from trade
partners, the Carter Administration did not make much of an
effort to educate the Congress and the American public to the
fact that the United States is itself not above reproach in the
area of trade barriers. Of course, such instruction would
have blunted the effectiveness of the Congressional threat as a
negotiating tool, and the STR found this tool too valuable to
sacrifice, even in the interests of truth. Instead, the STR
has allowed Congress to develop the impression that the other
GATT contracting parties are dragging their feet where free
trade is concerned and that the United States is the cheated
party. Thus, as the U.S. trade balance fails to correct itself,
and as the American economy spirals downward into a recession
with an accompanying increase in unemployment, the voices of
protectionism will be heard with increasing sympathy by
nervous American politicians.

    This discontent may soon crystallize into a broad political
coalition to chastise the scoundrels overseas. But the United
States will probably not bring its grievances to multilateral
forums; in fact, the most recent STR tack emphasizes bilateral
"reciprocity" over multilateral negotiations on the most favored
nation (MFN) principle.(3) The perception in Japan is that
the United States demands reciprocity only where it finds itself
at a disadvantage, while a genuine overall reciprocity is quite

another matter; for example, in such areas as dumping regulations and countervailing duties, where Japan is the injured party, the United States conveniently forgets its concern for reciprocity. The Japanese also feel that the United States is much more interested in restoring its trade equilibrium than in guaranteeing the openness of the world market. Therefore, the United States pressures Japan to increase American imports beyond "mere" reciprocity in order to compensate for the lack of effort on the part of American exporters. Finally, both the United States and Japan know that Japan will be more hurt than the United States by a bilateral trade war.

At this moment, it is impossible to determine which side is right and which side is wrong. On the one hand, it is difficult to prove the existence of Japan's alleged hidden trade barriers, but it is equally difficult to prove that such hidden barriers do not exist at all. It comes down to the fact that both sides tend to believe whatever is most comforting. The United States believes that its exports to Japan would increase if Japan would only remove its trade barriers and expand its economy. Japan believes that its trade barriers are certainly not more significant than those of the United States, and that American exports are hindered not by trade barriers but by the lack of long-term marketing expertise on the part of American exporters. Both contentions are based on a fair amount of truth.

One great consolation in the midst of this welter of half-truths and accusations is the fact that American pressure for Japan's trade liberalization ultimately serves both the international cause of trade expansion and the United States's own political interests. Obviously, the international community will side with the United States against Japan because many other countries share grievances over Japanese exporting practices, and these nations will automatically benefit from Japanese concessions to the United States without exerting direct pressure on Japan themselves. In addition, if the United States succeeds in obtaining these concessions, the Congressional push for protectionism will relent and the world can be reasonably assured of the stability of the international trade scene, at least for the time being.

Japan's guilt complex towards the United States over its laggard liberalization is nearly a thing of the past. Because the Japanese now believe that Japan's trade barriers compare well with those of the United States, the only driving force for further liberalization in Japan is the consumer interest. And here lies a new difficulty, for the secrets of Japan's past success - the cohesiveness of the private sector and the search for consensus in the determination of policy - are now becoming shackles against the initiation of bold new policy directions.

Given this immobilism in Japan, should the United States press more strongly for Japan's liberalization to redress the bilateral imbalance, or should it simply wait for further exchange rate changes to produce the same effect? As a matter of theory, unilateral trade concessions should always be preferred to exchange rate changes; trade concessions expand imports without reducing exports and therefore expand trade, while exchange rate changes reduce the surplus country's exports and have a neutral impact on world trade. But given the current impasse, we may have to rely on exchange rate changes to produce divisions within the Japanese camp, allowing an articulate liberal trade group to lobby actively for more substantive policy change.(4) One splinter in such a division is the Sangyo Keikaku Kondankai (Industrial Planning Council) - a private group of senior businessmen, conservative academics, and other influential people. This Council has been very vocal in its support of the idea that the stronger industries should be restrained in their export drive so that the weaker (and labor-intensive) domestic industries can survive. However, it does advocate selling the products of the labor-intensive industries to the less developed countries and those of the resource-intensive industries to the resource-rich nations. One more splinter, organized by industries supplying materials to other manufacturers, has recently introduced proposals to maintain the productive capacities of these resource-suppliers at an essential level, despite their diminished international competitiveness in the face of rising oil prices and the revaluation of the yen. However, this group's concern lies more in the area of national security, and therefore its proposals lead to the provision of only temporary trade relief. But the birth of these two groups is a welcome sign, in that they demonstrate the dawning recognition in Japan that a trade policy can benefit from public examination and vigorous debate. The Domei, the largest federation among the unions with a social democratic orientation, has lately become a strong advocate of increasing the access of agricultural imports to the Japanese market in the interests of the consumer. No clear-cut free trade group has emerged yet, but divisions are developing in the Japanese camp, and we can hope that the appeals of the protectionists will one day be met with organized, persistent, and compelling opposition from the advocates of liberalization.

In order to avert a collision between the United States and Japan over trade, a strategy for coping with the current economic strains in their relationship must be developed. First of all, more and better information must be disseminated to both the Japanese and the American publics, a process in which both governments should draw upon the knowledge of scholars and other experts in the field. This applies to almost all areas of the current dispute, from the porpoise and whale controversy to the question of steel and semiconductor trade. The provision of ample statistics and fact sheets may help to neutralize the emotionalizing tactics of the protectionist interests on both sides. (For example, see Table 4.1 for a demonstration of the multilateral and changeable nature of Japan's trade.)

One essential prerequisite for this process of education is much greater openness in Japan's method of policy formulation. Japanese policy makers have never had to face the sort of extensive congressional hearings that American officials confront, which offer a forum to proponents of widely varying points of view. Foreign observers, and even Japanese them- selves, have found it difficult to determine where Japanese government and business officials actually stand on the question of free trade. If Japan truly seeks more under- standing abroad, it must increase the visibility of its policy- making process, and must also provide an opportunity to domestic importers and foreign exporters (as well as domestic manufacturers, consumers, etc.) to present their various cases at official hearings. Proposals should be examined closely for the establishment of an Independent Trade Commission in Japan similar to the American ITC to investigate conditions of injury to domestic industries (or the threat thereof) and to scrutinize domestic industrial pleas for protection.

In the interest of effecting a change in Japanese priorities, the United States could help reduce the "hunger mentality" of Japan by concluding long-term subsistence level supply agreements on major commodities. Japan may also opt to diversify its supply sources and to enhance its global resource reach by investing in such countries as Brazil and Mexico. Both policies work in the same direction, that of relieving Japan's anxiety over the availability of resources, and thereby quenching its need for foreign currencies. However, the United States must not be perceived by the Japanese public as retaining complete control over the ultimate security "button" (whether it be a question of defense, food, or energy), for Japanese leadership will not be able to contain the surge of nationalism and hostility that would greet the clumsy and transparent employment of a linkage strategy.

Clearly both countries must make efforts to redress the bilateral trade imbalance. The United States should suggest - but should not impose - what it regards as the preferable mode for achieving greater equilibrium in trade with Japan. Politically it would be easier for Japan to restrain its export drive than to widen the avenue for imports; however, the Carter Administration has indicated that the United States would rather expand its exports to Japan than reduce its Japanese imports (which, in any event, has been occurring on a quantitative basis since April 1978). Both countries should

Table 4.1.   Japan's Merchandise Trade Balance
with its Major Trading Partners
(in millions of US dollars; exports, f.o.b.; imports, c.i.f.)
ranked by size of import value, 1977

Country	1971	1975	1977	1978
USA	+2,615	-376	+7,603	+10,428
Saudi Arabia	-616	-4,781	-6,206	-5,219
Australia	-1,032	-2,416	-2,979	-2,622
Indonesia	-401	-1,581	-3,221	-3,170
Iran	-1,127	-3,125	-2,327	-1,537
Canada	-127	-1,347	-1,173	-1,318
UAE	-166	-1,354	-1,916	-1,614
Kuwait	-335	-1,643	-1,560	-1,720
Korea	+584	+939	+1,953	+3,426
Malaysia	-170	-125	-709	-743
West Germany	+50	+521	+1,295	+1,673
Brunei	-1	-987	-1,384	-1,352
Taiwan	+637	+1,009	+1,227	+1,851
UK	+157	+662	+998	+970
Brazil	+13	+46	-107	+473
South Africa	+96	-7	-145	-71
Philippines	-51	-94	+204	+493
Oman	-77	-450	-778	-774
India	-168	-187	-298	-62
Thailand	+215	+235	+616	+692
China	+257	+729	+395	+1,029
USSR	-119	+457	+518	+1,076

SOURCE: International Monetary Fund, Direction   of   Trade,
Annual 1971-77, and Yearbook 1979, Washington D.C.,
1979.

coordinate their various strategies to redress the trade
imbalance so that the efforts of one government do not cancel
out those of the other. Already, some progress has been
made as a result of U.S. anti-inflationary policy and export
promotion, on the one hand, and Japan's reflation policy and
import facilitation program, on the other. The bilateral
contention regarding the exchange rate intervention has
subsided, as well, and as other policy measures are
coordinated, the stability of the exchange rate should be
enhanced. It is also important to establish principles for
future trade negotiations, regarding, for instance, reciprocity
and the MFN principle. A more equitable policy of sharing the
burdens of defense should be outlined before the tension over
Japan's "free ride" produces unfortunate repercussions in
trade, investment, and other areas.

The United States and Japan have too long been engaged
in a mirror war. Japan has too long depended upon foreign
pressure to force it to act in its own national interest. On
the other hand, the United States has depended too much on
the tactic of bullying Japan into action. In the past, when
the Japanese liberalization of trade had not yet affected the
hard-core agricultural commodities, and when the U.S. Congress had a clear leadership structure, the arrangement -
faulty as it was - worked. And when the American posture on
trade, energy, and international monetary affairs was more
multilateral in its focus, the United States enjoyed international
endorsement of its policies. These conditions do not obtain
anymore, and new environments will have to be created in both
countries to allow the voices of enlightened self-interest to
prevail.

NOTES

(1)   Thus Japan's current account surplus has become a topic
       for bilateral government conferences rather than IMF con-
       frontations, and the ill-fated commitment of the Japanese
       economy to a 7 percent growth rate in 1978 was made bi-
       laterally in January 1978 rather than at the OECD.
(2)   See, for example, the July 1978 proposal that the
       President impose a 5 percent surcharge on all Japanese
       imports, or the later passage by Congress of a prohi-
       bition against U.S. concessions on textile tariffs during
       the Multilateral Trade Negotiations (vetoed by President
       Carter).
(3)   If applied bilaterally, the reciprocity principle would mean
       that Japan should treat American products in Japan as
       the United States treats Japanese products in America;
       the MFN principle requires Japan to treat American prod-

ucts as it does France's (or any other country's) products. The U.S. - Canadian automotive agreement and the customs union aspects of the EEC infringe upon this basic principle of GATT.

(4) This activity can be supplemented by the creation of a Japan-U.S. trade council in Tokyo by the American government and business community.

5 Avoiding a U.S.—Japanese Collision

Akira Kojima

The past several years have witnessed a disturbing deterioration in the relationship between the United States and Japan. Some observers feel that the two countries may be heading for an Ice Age of sorts, brought on by the sunspots of their various economic and trade problems. Such an estrangement is indeed possible, although it is difficult to say how serious the possibility is in fact. At this point, all that is certain is the fact that an increase in the hostility between Japan and the United States cannot possibly benefit either party and will quite likely damage both nations severely.

At the present time, our economic difficulties are the focal point of concern in Washington and Tokyo. But we need to keep in mind the fact that the association between the United States and Japan involves a great deal more than trade matters, particularly in a world that is growing ever more interdependent. And even if we confine our attention entirely to economic issues, it is clear that our areas of common interest far outweigh our differences. Although the United States has indeed experienced a large imbalance in its trade with Japan, Japan still represents the largest single overseas market for American goods (U.S. exports to Japan totalled well over $13 billion in 1978), and America's trade with the nations of East Asia as a whole exceeds its trade with any other region of the world.(1) In addition, the return on American investments in East Asia in 1978 was the highest in the world, and the trend is continuing upward, even while a vast array of natural resources still remains to be developed in the area. In general, both Japan and the United States are already working jointly towards common goals along a broad range of problems, and neither can achieve these goals on its own; the Mutual Security Treaty between the two countries comes to mind as the foremost example of the extent of their involvement with each other.

As a Japanese journalist based in the United States, I would like to offer a few perceptions about the relationship between our two countries, stressing above all the often-ignored necessity for considering numerous elements – both short- and long-term features of the relationship, as well as the cyclical, structural, historical, social, and cultural factors impinging upon the current difficulties between the United States and Japan.

Perhaps as a result of these tensions, a number of books about Japan have appeared recently in the United States, and are gaining a wide audience among the American public. But it would be well to remember that this apparently widespread interest in Japan is a relatively new phenomenon in America. Ten years ago, Professor Mastaka Kosaka noted that Arthur Schlesinger's history of the Kennedy Administration, A Thousand Days, contained not a single reference to Japan. When the trade dispute occurred in the early 1970s, it might be said to have sprung full-blown before an American public which neither knew nor, presumably, cared very much about the other party in the quarrel. On the other hand, the Japanese have for years been struggling to understand the United States. Mike Mansfield, U.S. Ambassador to Japan, has described this lopsided relationship as a sort of telescope through which the United States and Japan look at each other, Japan seeing a huge but detailed America through the eyepiece, and the United States seeing a shrunken version of Japan at the other end. To most Americans, according to Mr. Mansfield, Japan does not seem all that significant, and therefore the United States tends to undervalue the importance of the Japanese nation, people, and culture. Thus one might say that the flow of information between our two countries is just as unbalanced as our trade flow – but in the opposite direction.

This information gap arises partly because the internationalization of Japan has occurred exclusively through the medium of trade. While Japan has been carrying on international trade of gigantic proportions, it has done almost nothing in the area of cultural exchange, and this pattern of trade without cultural exchange has been characteristic of Japan throughout its history. No doubt this lopsided exchange has become one of the principal sources of misunderstanding and conflict between Japan and the United States. Japan desperately needs to narrow this gap if it is to obtain the respect and understanding of American policy makers and of the American public. Otherwise, American demands, prompted by uninformed domestic pressure groups, may unknowingly push the Japanese into deepening hostility toward the United States and irreparably damage what has been a very close and beneficial relationship for both countries.

In order to avoid this situation, both Japan and the
United States must struggle to rectify the presently excessive
imbalance of trade. But the American public needs to
understand that this imbalance is not entirely the product of
Japanese economic aggression. They must recognize the fact
that the balance derives partly from a cyclical element -
namely, the divergence in the rates of inflation and economic
growth in both countries. Also, and even more important, the
current positions of the United States and Japan represent the
inevitable results of a historical process that governs the
evolution of any nation's balance of payments.

At the first stage of this process of evolution, a country
may run a large deficit in its balance of trade, and this deficit
is usually financed abroad by some means such as international
borrowing or special economic assistance. With its industry in
its infant phase during this first stage of industrial
development, this country might adopt various protective
measures, such as tariffs, import quotas, and subsidies to
domestic industries, to defend its domestic industries against
foreign competition until they grow to the point where they
can be more competitive internationally. Such measures are
intended, theoretically, to be temporary, and are supposed to
be removed when the country achieves the next phase in its
economic evolution, characterized by surpluses in its
international trade. The trade liberalization begun in the
second stage is continued and even heightened in the third
stage of evolution, as the surpluses earned by the export
efforts of the nation's now highly competitive industries are
channeled into direct and indirect investment overseas. In the
fourth stage of this process, the nation will probably
experience a trade deficit as a result of competition from
countries with lower wages or higher productivity. When a
developed country makes direct investments in overseas
factories, its domestic industries must necessarily encounter
increased competition in both export markets and domestic
markets, as its products vie with those of foreign industries
which the fourth-stage nation helped to establish. This trade
deficit can, however, be covered by remitting incomes earned
by direct and indirect investments overseas.

It is evident that Japan is currently in the third stage of
its balance of payments evolution, while the United States has
already entered its fourth stage. For this reason, it is
obviously misleading to focus only upon trade figures as an
expression of the economic relations between the two countries.
A recent article in The Washington Monthly reminds us of the
significance of this pattern of evolution with respect to the
ailing American steel industry:

In 1901, a group of British steel executives visited
the United States and was awed by the pace of in-

novation and growth in our steel industry. In 30
years, the American industry has changed from an
infant, with an output only one-sixth that of the
dominant Britain, to a giant, whose output was
double that of the British industry . . . . Three-
quarters of a century later, the American steel industry is politely termed a "mature" industry . . . .
Meanwhile, American markets are threatened by
steel-makers from across the sea: the Japanese
. . . . As their troubles have mounted, American
steel executives have tended to blame everyone but
themselves.(2)

In 1978, after a period of hard negotiations, Japan and
the United States established the "reference price" formula for
steel, thereby effectively increasing the price of imported
Japanese steel by 15 percent. Washington must have hoped
that this breathing space would enable American firms to
expand their share of the steel market; instead, however, the
steel industry increased its prices, thereby fueling inflation
and losing ground in the steel market to newly industrialized
countries like Brazil and Korea. This turn of events
demonstrates the deteriorating entrepreneurship of the
American steel industry, but, even more important, it
underlines the fact that the patterns of economic development
occur on a global scale and involve every country in the
world. Both the United States and Japan stand at a transition
point in this process. The United States will probably be
entering a new stage of evolution, which will most likely be
characterized by increasing economic global interdependence
with a corresponding decrease in the importance of national
sovereignty; the European Community represents a kind of
experiment in this direction. The United States should attempt
to match the pace of its foreign investment to its balance of
payments, and should also encourage much more investment in
its domestic industries. The physical plant of the U.S.
industrial sector is in bad need of long-term capital
investment. For example, it is shocking to discover that until
very recently, the fifth largest steel manufacturer in the
United States, Inland Steel, hadn't built a new blast furnace
since World War II. On the other hand, Japan, having
reached the transition from the third to the fourth phase of
evolution, should expand its direct and indirect overseas
investment. The controversial "Jones Report,"(3) summarizing
the findings and recommendations of the U.S. - Japan Task
Force of the House of Representatives, suggested that Japan
invest in American manufacturing in order to "maintain
competitiveness in the U.S. markets," noting that this
investment would also help to rectify the trade imbalance.

The deterioration of the American manufacturing sector has been noted as one obvious cause of tension between Japan and the United States, as many inefficiently produced American goods fare badly in the marketplace. This unfortunate circumstance also adds to the domestic pressure in the United States for a return to protectionist trade policies. In particular, the American labor movement is a very powerful advocate of the hard-nosed approach in trade negotiations. Labor unions exert a disproportionate amount of political power in the United States; union membership has been declining in recent years, due largely to the restructuring of American industry. The ratio of union membership to the total working population of the United States declined from 26 percent in 1953 to 23 percent in 1968, and more recent figures indicate that organized labor actually lost 600,000 members during the 1974-76 period. Furthermore, the traditional industries - such as steel and textile manufacturing - which happen to be less competitive, have much higher ratios of union membership among their workers, while the technologically advanced industries, which are much more competitive internationally, employ a relatively lower proportion of union members.(4) The decline in union membership is likely to continue, as more and more American workers enter the high technology and service industries. Thus the concentration of union members in the less competitive sectors of the American economy will only strengthen the already powerful strain of protectionism in the labor movement, at the same time that the unions will actually come to represent a numerically smaller portion of the American electorate.

Japan faces a similar problem in the disproportionate political influence of its textile industry, which has forced the continuation of a number of protectionist measures and therefore has retarded its own adjustment to the international economic situation. But the power of the labor movement is deeply entrenched in American politics, and, in the case of trade with Japan, the labor movement joins forces with the less competitive American industries to exert tremendous pressure upon the United States government to take actions which can only jeopardize the U.S. - Japanese relationship.

Threatened by Japan's international competitiveness and fearing losses in profits and increases in unemployment, American special interests and politicians lash out against the Japanese, and become impatient with the apparent Japanese reluctance to respond to American demands. In many cases, the reluctance is real, but many Americans do not understand the amount of time it takes for Japan to develop new policies. In Japan, it is ironically said that most high-ranking officials are men of inaction. To some extent this is true, partly because in Japan an individual's advancement depends largely upon the ability to avoid making errors. In a nation in which human resources are expendable, a single error can be fatal to one's career; thus inaction often seems preferable to the risk of mistaken action. This tendency in Japan's leadership is abetted by the need in Japanese society for consensus. The government often fails to take initiatives because a consensus has not yet developed for them among the Japanese public. Americans do not understand that official Japanese policy may follow one line, while, at the same time, momentum is developing among the people for a shift in the opposite direction. Once the impetus for change has gathered general support, government policy changes to reflect it, and, in the process, appears to swing from one extreme to another, while in reality the consensus for change has been building for some time.(5) Irked by Japan's apparent inertia and confused by these occasional and startling swings of the pendulum, the United States has tended in the past to prod Japan into acting by administering a form of shock treatment to produce radical changes in the public mood. For example, in 1971, the so-called Nixon Shock jolted Japan, and suddenly the American media proclaimed a crisis in U.S. - Japanese relations.

This policy of shocking Japan into action can prove dangerous. Japan has been developing a sense of greater national autonomy in recent years. In itself, this represents a positive turn of events, but it has been accompanied lately by a growing resentment over Japan's long submission to American leadership and a deepening hostility toward that leadership. In addition, American officials have not taken the most felicitous approach to dealing with Japan. Their attitude has in general been arrogant, conveying the message that Japan needs the United States much more than the United States needs Japan. In the light of this combination of Japanese resentment and American insistence, Japan's apparent propensity to swing from one end of the pendulum's arc to the other without much warning at the official level does not bode well for future relations between the two countries.

Most disturbingly, Japan's thirty-year-old policies favoring internationalism and opposing militarism may be placed in jeopardy. Recent opinion polls suggest that there exists the real possibility in Japan of a swing of public sentiment toward isolationism, protectionism, and rearmament. Michael Pillsbury's provocative essay, "A Japanese Card?"(6) argues that there is an odd contrast in Japan between the official line on defense and the present reality, and he contends that Japan will soon return to its former status as a military power. As he analyzes it, the nature of official discussion on national security issues has changed lately, and, for the first time in thirty years, the Japanese are not being shy about defense. Many elements make up the background for the change which Mr. Pillsbury astutely perceives in Japanese attitudes towards defense. The concern over economic security after the oil crisis some years ago triggered widespread concern about defense. The growing threat of the Soviet Union and the political turmoil in Indochina also contributed to this change. The generational shift has had a great deal to do with this development: the generation born after World War II is currently coming of age. These young people outnumber their elders, and, not having experienced the miseries of wartime Japan, they tend to be more amenable to the idea of Japan's rearmament.

Many - Mr. Pillsbury among them - argue that this is a healthy sign, and that it would benefit both Japan and the United States if Japan were to rearm. I disagree. The upswing of militarism in Japan will have negative consequences for Japan, for its neighbors in East Asia, and for the United States as well. Perhaps the American people do not realize that Japan is the world's third largest national economy and ranks seventh in total military spending. In The Fragile Blossom, Zbigniew Brzezinski cited four sources of pressure upon Japan to become a major military power once again: the feeling of external threat, the need to protect overseas economic interests, the rise of nationalism, and the decline of confidence in the American nuclear guarantee.(7) By administering shock treatments to Japan in the form of confrontations over trade, the United States will push the Japanese public into both an increase in nationalism and an increase in distrust of the United States. It is likely that such shocks may also do little to alleviate Japan's sense of external threat and its concern over foreign economic interests. In short, such activities on the part of the United States could quite possibly fulfill the conditions that would lead Japan to seek military power. And to anyone who lived in Japan during the last war, that possibility is very frightening.

It is essential that relations between Japan and the United States be safeguarded against further shock and mayhem; it is also important that this relationship not be taken for granted. Momentary differences, no matter how bitter they may be, are not worth the estrangements they can cause. The world economy never stands still; it moves in a constant process of evolution which necessarily produces friction, tension, and even conflict. The trade problems between Japan and the United States must be regarded as the inevitable results of this process. In particular, the American public must keep in mind the fact that the long-term historical perspective casts events into a light very different from that of the short term. While trying to buy time for the evolutions they are undergoing, the United States and Japan must do whatever they can to repair the damage that has already been done. The trade imbalance will continue to preoccupy the two governments, but they must also rectify the huge imbalance of information between them, so that each may understand the other's problems and modes of action. In the end, the endeavor to avert a collision between the United States and Japan may prove painful and costly, but it can neither hurt nor cost both countries nearly as much as the collision itself.

NOTES

(1) See for example W. Robert Warne, "U.S. Economic Role in East Asia," The U.S. Role in a Changing World Political Economy: Major Issues for the 96th Congress (Washington, D.C.: Government Printing Office, 1979), pp. 371-85.
(2) "Who Killed the Steel Industry - The Unions, the Company, the Government, or All of the Above?" The Washington Monthly, March 1979.
(3) U.S. Congress, House Subcommittee on Trade, Task Force on United States-Japan Trade, 95th Congress (Washington, D.C.: Government Printing Office, January 2, 1979).
(4) This information is based on a report delivered by Ronald E. Berenbeim at a Conference Board seminar on the future of American labor unions, in New York in March 1979.
(5) For an enlightening discussion of the role of consensus in Japanese society, see Shichihei Yamamoto's Kuuki no Kenkyuu (A Study of Atmosphere) (Tokyo: Bungei Shunju, 1977).
(6) Michael Pillsbury, "A Japanese Card?" Foreign Policy, Winter 1978-79, pp. 3-30.
(7) Zbigniew Brzezinski, The Fragile Blossom (New York: Harper and Row, 1979), p. 97.

II

Sources of Competition in U.S.—Japanese Relations: Differences in Corporate Conduct

6 American and Japanese Industrial Structures: A Sectoral Comparison
Masahisa Naitoh

It is commonly understood that the economic problems between the United States and Japan arise from a variety of factors: the large trade imbalance, the rapid appreciation of the yen and the undervaluation of the dollar, the differing economic growth rates of the two countries, and related matters. However, many of these phenomena can be regarded as natural consequences of disparities in the industrial structures of the two countries as they have developed since the end of World War II.

Let us look first at Japan. The Japanese industrial sector can be divided into two portions: the basic and material input industries (steel, petrochemicals, etc.) on the one hand, and the assembling-processing industries (automobiles, televisions, etc.) on the other. Since World War II, the driving force behind the high growth rate of the Japanese economy as a whole has been the cycle of accelerating investment in the basic and material industries. The remarkable growth of these industries has proceeded in an unbalanced manner in relation to that of the assembling-processing industries in Japan, whose slow (but steady) growth has depended upon the availability of skilled labor and upon export demand. By contrast, the basic and material input industries were able, until the early 1970s, to realize tremendous economies of scale because of the seemingly unlimited availability of money for capital-intensive investment, and because of the tremendous technological advances of the postwar period. However, after the oil crisis in 1973, sluggish worldwide demand and environmental restrictions on industrial activity in Japan imposed limits upon the expansion of the basic industries. That sector of the Japanese economy became depressed, a situation which has led to reductions in the importation of raw materials into the country. On the

other hand, the energy crisis has had a much smaller impact
upon the assembling-processing sector of the economy, since
these industries are relatively labor-intensive, and their
products are highly differentiated. World demand for the high
quality goods produced by Japanese workers has grown at the
same time that Japan's imports of raw materials have levelled
off. For this reason, Japan has been experiencing a large
trade surplus and a reduced rate of economic growth - both of
which have become the targets of criticism by a number of
other countries, the most vocal of which has of course been
the United States.

   In contrast, American industry during the postwar era
has been characterized by a low level of fixed investment and
a consequent lag in the adoption of new technologies. As a
result, a significant proportion of the plant of the basic and
material input industries in the United States has become
obsolete. The reluctance of American industry to face the
need to change its attitudes regarding fixed investment and
consumer demand helps to explain the fact that American
products have been losing ground in the Japanese market at a
time when European commodities have actually increased their
share in that market. Thus the deterioration of the American
balance of payments position vis-a-vis Japan has its origins in
the different behaviors of the American and Japanese industrial
sectors since 1945. It is a significant and heartening
development that during the course of the recent bilateral
discussions regarding Japan's trade surplus, the United States
has begun to consider the need for policies that promote
domestic investment and technology in order to rehabilitate the
American industrial sector.

   In the United States, industrial structure is simply an
expression of the aggregate of all industrial activities
occurring at any given time; it is described and expressed
statistically. In the Japanese case, industrial structure is
much more elaborate, at least as far as the manufacturing
sector is concerned: the Japanese view industrial structure as
a system for setting and implementing goals for both public
and private sectors. In the United States, of course,
industrial structure is occasionally viewed in systematic terms,
but it is seldom perceived as a set of objectives or specific
targets. This difference in perception between our two
countries is reflected in operational differences in behavior and
policy, as individual industries cope with periods of recession
or as they face a decline in their own competitiveness.

   Industries in the United States and Japan view themselves
differently as they undergo structural changes over time.
Individual industries go through developmental stages: an
infant stage is succeeded by a high growth stage, which is
followed by a senescent stage. Japanese industries in the past
have received protection from competition during their infant

stages.   Generally, they ask for continued protection even
after entering the high growth stage.   When this protection is
denied to them because of foreign pressure, they focus all
their efforts on maintaining the high growth stage for as long
as possible.   They adopt a long-term perspective and invest
heavily   in   new   facilities   embodying   highly   advanced
technology.   When they arrive at the senescent stage, they
accept "death" relatively easily, as the cooperation of all the
companies concerned is enlisted to minimize the disruptions
resulting from the industry's demise.

Quite the opposite is true of the United States: American
industries resist death fiercely, and it is during the senescent,
and not the infant, stage of their life cycle that their demand
for protection becomes most pronounced.   Protectionism appears
to be a viable alternative to corporate death in American industry because of the sheer size of the U.S. domestic market,
which is large enough (so American industries reason) to support industries that cannot compete with foreign goods in
overseas markets.   Indeed, the prospect of being safeguarded
by protectionism in their "old age" may help to explain the
relatively undynamic behavior of U.S. industries during their
high growth stage: the need to maintain the conditions for high
growth is felt less strongly if the industry assumes that it will
be able to survive indefinitely after the onset of senescence.

If industrial structure is viewed in the Japanese way, as
a mechanism for setting and meeting economic goals, three
factors stand out over all others in shaping the industrial
sector.   They are 1) changing human needs, the source of
economic demand; 2) technological innovation, which brings
both   new   products   and   new   production   processes   into
existence;   and   3)   the   international   economic   environment,
which, in the case of Japan, must provide a stable and
inexpensive supply of raw materials as well as a large export
market.   Japanese businesses are very sensitive to the first
and third of these factors, and strive to be as adaptable as
possible to change.   The effects of this attitude can be seen
in   the   shifts   which   have   occurred   in   the   structure   of
U.S.-Japanese trade since 1960.   The composition of Japanese
exports to the United States has changed much more over the
years than the composition of American exports to Japan.   For
example, between 1960 and 1977, the share of machinery among
Japan's total exports to the United States increased from 17.1
percent to 68 percent, while, at the same time, textiles fell
from 26.6 percent to 3 percent.   The structure of American
exports to Japan has changed less drastically, the share of
raw materials and fuels increasing from 7.9 percent to 21.8
percent, and manufactures, from 33.1 percent to 37 percent.
The relatively greater dynamism of the Japanese export sector
suggests that Japanese companies have made more of an effort
than their American counterparts to adapt to consumer needs

and to reorient their activities to a changing economic situation.

When the analysis is extended to the economy as a whole, however, important qualifications become necessary. In Japan, the manufacturing sector is very efficient, but the primary and tertiary sectors of the economy are highly inefficient. The situation in the United States is completely reversed - the secondary sector is the least efficient of the three. As a whole, the Japanese economy actually functions less efficiently than that of the United States, and also less efficiently than that of West Germany, France, or England.

The disparity in performance among economic sectors is one explanation for the overvaluation of the yen relative to its real purchasing power. The exchange rate tends to be set by the comparative costs of tradeable goods. It therefore reflects the relationship of the Japanese and American manufacturing sectors - in other words, the relationship between the most efficient economic sector in Japan and the least efficient sector in the United States.

Let me discuss briefly some of the characteristics of the Japanese primary and tertiary sectors. Japanese primary industry accounts for 12.6 percent of the total labor force, a high proportion compared to the U.S. figure of 4 percent. This sector, especially its agricultural component, functions as a reservoir of disguised unemployment in Japan and is one of Japan's chief concerns in the area of manpower policy. The slow pace of change in Japanese agriculture reflects the relative fixity of Japanese dietary habits - a pattern particularly at odds with the rapid changes in other consumer tastes that have accompanied economic growth. To some foreign observers, Japanese agriculture appears to perform well, because Japan's rate of food self-sufficiency is 70 percent despite its relatively poor agricultural resources. Still, America's agricultural efficiency far exceeds that of Japan. And the level of protection enjoyed by Japanese agriculture is among the highest in the world, ranking alongside that of Switzerland and Sweden. In view of Japan's role in the world economy, it is crucial now that Japan adjust to the global agricultural situation. American farmers have taken what amounts to a free-trade stance, one which, if emulated by farmers in other countries, would greatly aid the world economy. Therefore, the possibility of U.S.-Japanese cooperation in matters of agricultural trade has acquired a great significance, and the recent discussions between our two countries regarding beef, citrus, and other foodstuffs represent an important step in this direction.

With respect to the service sector of the two economies, the tertiary sector contributes 59 percent of the total value added to the Japanese economy, compared to 62.2 percent in the United States. The probable reasons for the higher American ratio are the size of the transportation industry (a function of the sheer size of the country), the size of the military sector, and the higher level of research and development endeavors and of services generally in the United States. However, since 1970 the Japanese tertiary sector has exceeded the secondary sector in its rate of investment growth. Thus even Japan's tertiary sector is now in the process of approaching American levels. This means that Japan's outmoded system of distributing commodities is being modernized - if only gradually, given the tenacity of the historical, cultural, and social obstacles to this process.

Leaving aside the still considerable differences between the primary and tertiary sectors of the Japanese and American economies, it is of course the great disparity in the secondary sectors of these two countries which has contributed most to Japan's current trade advantage, and hence to its current difficulties with the United States. The postwar development of the secondary industrial structure in Japan is worth looking at in greater detail, with particular emphasis upon the basic and material input industries that provided the motor for Japan's economic recovery.

From the end of the war until the mid-1950s, both government and private enterprise in Japan concentrated upon fostering such basic industries as steel and coal. These industries were viewed as strategic elements in the effort to revive a war-devastated economy and to lay the foundations for sustained industrial growth in the future. From the mid-1950s to the mid-1960s, this focus was broadened to include other heavy industries as well; automobiles, industrial machinery, electronics, and other assembling industries were given particular emphasis along with steel, petrochemicals, and other basic industries. These industries were singled out because they realized large economies of scale, their impact on other industries was considerable, their capacity for manpower absorption was large, and their elasticity of income to demand was high. During this period, Japanese corporations depended heavily on external financing. A steady supply of investment capital was in fact available, thanks largely to the high savings rate of the Japanese economy and the flexibility of the banking system in meeting corporate needs. As a result, the Japanese economy maintained high levels of fixed investment, which permitted a considerable expansion of capacity and encouraged the adoption of the newest production technologies in steel, petrochemicals, and other industries.

Around the mid-1960s, however, a new goal emerged for the Japanese economy, expressed in the popular slogan of "informationalizing industry": it meant, essentially, the computerization of industrial activities at the managerial and industrial levels. The main theme of this period was (to use

Daniel Bell's terminology) the transition from "industrial" to "postindustrial" society. This notion was carried over into the 1970s, under a new slogan - the "knowledge intensification" of industry. But in fact, after 1970, the domestic and international environment changed drastically, and it became clear that our economy was reaching a critical turning point in its rate of growth (see Table 6.1). It became impossible to pursue the target of "knowledge intensification" as consistently as had been hoped. The changes on the international scene are well known: the collapse of the IMF system, the energy crisis, and the pressure from other countries regarding Japan's trade surplus. The domestic front in Japan saw the emergence, among other problems, of public concern over pollution and conservation. Many productive facilities developed overcapacities because of the sluggish economy, and differentials in international competitiveness widened among various Japanese industries because of the rapid appreciation of the yen.

Table 6.1. Rates of Growth in Output
in the United States and Japan
(Changes from previous year in real terms)

	1973	1974	1975	1976	1977	1978
United States	5.5	-1.4	-1.3	6.0	4.9	3.75
Japan	9.8	-1.3	2.4	6.0	5.1	5.5

SOURCES: International Monetary Fund Annual Report, 1977 and OECD Economic Outlook, no. 23, July 1978.

These problems have contributed to the current split in the Japanese secondary industrial sector between the sluggishness and overcapacity of basic industry on the one hand, and the relative vigor and strong export orientation of the assembling-processing industries on the other. Compared with the second half of 1973 - Japan's peak period of economic activity before the energy crisis - the production indices for the assembling-processing industries (e.g., office and farm machinery, automobiles, watches) in 1978 ranged between 130 percent and 300 percent of 1973 levels. By contrast, production in steel, nonferrous metals, chemical fertilizers, wood products, and other resource-dependent industries dropped to between 84 percent and 94 percent of 1973 levels. And the assembly industries which are heavily dependent upon capital investment - such as textiles, shipbuilding, and metalworking machinery - were still worse off, sinking to between 34 percent and 68 percent of their 1973 figures as a result of lagging investment. This pattern has given rise to the impression among Japan's trading partners that the Japanese economy is highly oriented toward exports. In fact, however, 1977 figures show that the ratio of exports to gross national product was 11.8 percent for Japan, in comparison to 23 percent for West Germany, 26 percent for the United Kingdom, and 6.4 percent for the United States. In the per capita value of its exports, Japan ranked thirty-second out of ninety-six countries; the United States, in thirty-fifth place, was not far behind. These figures suggest that the alleged export dependency of the Japanese economy is not really that much greater than that of the United States (see Table 6.2). The problem with Japan's exports is, quite simply, that those Japanese industries which happen to be most export-oriented compete strongly with their counterparts in other countries, offering products of higher quality for their cost.

It must also be remembered that traditional theories of international economics (as reflected in the Hechscher-Olin Theorem) focus only upon finished products, neglecting trade in semifinished products. Through the utilization of technological advances, industries producing semifinished goods, such as steel products, have become a major component of Japan's industrial structure. As a result, Japan has not needed to import semifinished products, and these items have instead assumed a significant place among Japanese exports.

A country's pattern of foreign trade is largely conditioned by its industrial structure. Japan's industrial structure is what has been called "semicomplete." Although raw materials are lacking, all further stages of the production process - from semifinished products to finished goods - are fully developed. An interesting contrast to Japan is Canada, which happens to be the country most intimately connected with the United States through trade. Canada's industrial structure is incomplete where Japan's is semicomplete; Canada exports raw materials to the United States, imports semifinished products, and both exports and imports finished products. Thus, the Canadian and U.S. industrial structures are complementary in terms of their implications for trade relations, while the Japanese and U.S. industrial structures are competitive. But the competition which characterizes U.S.-Japan trade relations must be seen as a product of the combined effects of vigorous investment in Japanese basic industries, on the one hand, and

Table 6.2. Dependence on Trade:
Japan and the United States

USA	Total Imports/GNP(%)	Japanese Imports/GNP(%)	Total Exports/GNP(%)	Exports to Japan/GNP(%)	Japanese Imports/person
1976	7.1	0.9	6.8	0.6	$ 72
1977	7.8	0.9	6.4	0.6	$ 86
1978	8.1	1.1	6.6	0.6	$112

JAPAN	Total Imports/GNP(%)	US Imports/GNP(%)	Total Exports/GNP(%)	Exports to US/GNP(%)	US Imports/person
1976	11.5	2.1	11.9	2.8	$104
1977	10.3	1.8	11.7	2.9	$105
1978	8.1	1.5	9.9	2.5	$129

SOURCES: U.S. Department of Commerce, Bureau of the Census; Japanese Ministry of Finance, Bureau of Customs.

the loss of innovative spirit among American industries on the other. The criticism of Japan for not importing more finished products is beside the point.

It is also relevant to observe that Japan has been a very obedient student of the American business system. In seeking economic recovery after World War II, Japan introduced mass production, mass distribution, and mass consumption ideas from the United States. Given the existence of large markets at home as well as in America and Europe, the Japanese worked effectively to apply American business ideas and emphasize the development of such consumer-oriented industries as autos and consumer electronics. By contrast, West Germany took the path of fostering the machine-tool and other industries which were not competitive with U.S. industry. This is one reason why, even though Germany's trade surplus trend is similar to Japan's, the voices of pressure groups in the United States have been raised most loudly against Japan. (See Table 6.3 for a listing of the trade balances of the major economic powers and blocs for selected years from 1965 to 1978.)

The most problematic sector in the Japanese economy today is basic industry, whose unbalanced growth and overexpansion in the past have led us to the present lag in natural resource imports and fixed investment. Between 1960 and 1976, Japanese steel production capacity increased 6.9 times, compared to 1.12 times in the United States, 1.9 times in West Germany, and 3.79 times in Italy. The dramatic expansion of Japanese basic industry relied upon a stable supply of natural resources, stable foreign exchange rates, and an international environment conducive to free trade. By the early 1970s, however, this expansion had stalled as a result of environmentalist constraints at home, the energy crisis, and the world recession that followed. As the 1980s begin, Japan faces the problem of adjusting its overexpanded basic industry sector to the realities of the supply and demand gap in the world, the rapid strides of many underdeveloped countries, and the requirements of Japan's role in the world economy.

Another basic problem of the Japanese economy is the discontinuity between the productive structure and the manpower structure. Japan's economic growth has been characterized by the allocation of capital to the capital-intensive basic industries and the allocation of labor to the traditional sectors, such as agriculture and distribution, which absorbed the large redundant portion of our work force. One result is that these sectors enjoy a degree of political power disproportionate to their economic role, thanks to their control of votes and their skillful use of traditional social and political relationships.

Industries must adjust to both structural and cyclical economic change. The most serious problems of adjustment are

Table 6.3. World Trade Balance,* 1965, 1970, 1973-78
(in billions of US dollars)

Area/Country	1965	1970	1973	1974	1975	1976	1977	1978**
Developed countries	-6.9	- 9.6	-16.2	-60.7	-27.6	-54.2	-58.5	-32.0
USA	4.3	.8	- 2.2	- 9.5	4.2	-14.6	-36.3	-39.4
Canada	- .2	2.5	1.7	.1	- 2.1	.2	1.3	1.8
Japan	.3	.4	- 1.4	- 6.5	- 2.1	2.4	9.8	18.5
EEC	-4.5	- 3.9	- 4.4	-19.0	- 3.5	-16.8	- 7.7	- 0.7
France	.2	- 1.0	- 1.1	- 6.7	.8	- 7.2	- 5.5	- 2.4
West Germany	.3	4.3	12.7	19.7	15.2	13.7	16.6	20.5
Italy	- .2	- 1.8	- 5.6	-10.6	- 3.6	- 6.2	- 2.5	- 0.3
UK	-2.3	- 2.4	- 8.2	-15.6	- 9.6	- 9.9	- 6.4	- 6.9
Other developed countries	-6.8	- 9.4	- 9.9	-25.8	-24.1	-25.5	-25.7	-12.0
Developing countries	-1.8	- 2.3	7.0	53.4	14.3	41.3	34.2	4.5
OPEC	4.2	7.6	19.3	87.0	58.9	71.2	60.1	40.7
Other	-6.0	- 9.9	-12.3	-33.6	-44.6	-29.9	-25.9	-36.2
Centrally planned economies	.5	.5	- .9	- 3.7	-10.4	- 6.0	.5	-
USSR	.1	1.1	.3	2.5	- 3.7	- .9	4.3	4.0
Eastern Europe	.2	- .4	- 1.1	- 4.7	- 6.0	- 6.1	- 4.8	- 3.7
China	.2	- .2	- .2	- .7	- .2	1.3	1.0	- 0.1
TOTAL ***	-8.2	-11.4	-10.2	-11.0	-23.7	-18.9	-23.8	-27.5

*Exports f.a.s. less imports c.i.f.
**Preliminary.
***Asymmetries arise in global payments aggregation because of discrepancies in coverage, classification, timing, and valuation in the recording of transactions by the countries involved.

SOURCE: The 1979 Annual Report of the Council of Economic Advisers (Washington, D.C.: Government Printing Office, January 24, 1979), p. 303.

those faced by structurally declining industries. In Japan these can be divided into three groups:

1) Industries declining in competitiveness because of the rapid appreciation of the yen and the increased competitiveness of the developing countries. Examples are textiles, chemical fertilizers, and shipbuilding. For these industries, the approach of the senescent stage has been spurred by changes in the international economy. If they are to survive, they will be able to do so only by relying on their ability to meet consumer needs through offering increasingly sophisticated and specialized products.

2) Industries operating below the break-even point because of the rapid increase in factor costs resulting from greatly increased energy prices. Such industries include aluminum and petrochemicals. Since there is no possibility of a reduction in energy prices to their earlier level, these industries will have to reduce productive capacity in accord with demand.

3) Overcapacity industries such as flat-furnace steel, which invested very heavily in the past, anticipating that high growth rates would continue indefinitely.

The adjustment of structurally declining industries must aim at restoring the balance between supply and demand. In a situation of generally lower economic growth, efforts by declining industries to adjust to structural change naturally face severe difficulties. The Japanese government therefore has enacted a Sluggish Industries Stabilization - Temporary Measures Act in order to facilitate the speedy reorganization and reconversion of structurally depressed industries with a minimum of disruption. The act provides for government loan guarantees for the purpose of purchasing and reconverting excess capacity. The ideas behind this measure are identical to those expressed in the resolution adopted at the OECD ministerial-level meeting in June, 1978. This resolution urged that, in response to import competition, all countries should avoid protectionism and instead adopt positive industrial adjustment policies through the modernization and rationalization of their industrial structure.

In Japan, the adjustments already made have been drastic. The shipbuilding industry has decided to reduce its capacity by 40 percent; aluminum, by one-third. The chemical fertilizer industry has recently seen a decision to scrap the biggest and newest ammonium plant in the world. Nippon Steel is now discussing the possible contraction and drastic rationalization of its Kawaishi factory.

In their economic implications, the cutbacks in the Japanese shipbuilding, aluminum, and chemical fertilizer industries are no less consequential than the closings of steel plants in Youngstown, Ohio. Yet the contrast between the Japanese and American reactions to these developments is striking. The Japanese companies, realizing that they had declined in international competitiveness, did their best to absorb the shock and cope with their difficulties by cooperating with each other and with other industries. Unlike their American counterparts, they did not criticize their foreign competitors, nor did they seek governmental protection from competition. Surely American industry would be in much healthier shape today if American companies could behave in a similar manner.

Industries must also adjust to cyclical economic change. In Japan, cartels are used for this purpose - for, unlike Americans, the Japanese do not regard all cartels as wrong. The Japanese Anti-Trust Act provides that under certain conditions cartels may be formed to restrict production, limit sales volume, and set prices. These conditions are fulfilled when: 1) the selling price of the products of an industry falls below the average cost of production for the industry as a whole; 2) there is difficulty in maintaining an adequate level of business; and 3) rationalization is not sufficient to cope with these difficulties. The Anti-Trust Act also provides that cartels may engage in the restriction of technology and product varieties and in the joint use of warehouse and transportation facilities and materials purchasing agents.

The Japanese Anti-Trust Act was introduced from the United States after World War II, but the provisions mentioned above were added several years later in order to adapt the Act to Japanese traditions. In the Japanese way of thinking, it is acceptable and natural for companies to cooperate with each other in order to cope with common difficulties. But in the absence of a cartel situation, competition in Japanese industry is generally more severe than in American industry. U.S. companies don't feel the need to form cartels in part because they are not so intensely competitive in the first place. The severe competition among Japanese industries is a reflection of the general competitiveness of Japanese society - a cultural trait which is a reaction to scarcity in a highly overpopulated land. However, it is fortunate that competitiveness coexists with a willingness to cooperate in order to permit adjustment to change.

These differences in industrial structure have their foundation in the divergent social values of our two cultures. It is a commonplace that Japanese social values are collectivistic, whereas those of the United States are individualistic - indeed, individualistic in a much "purer" sense than is true of Europe. The essence of American individualism lies in the goal of being independent and strong, while the essence of Japanese collectivism lies in the consciousness of helplessness and the desire to be loved. Because Americans place special value upon independence, they attach little importance to the notion of economic planning, which would subordinate that independence to the coordination of public and private efforts. The American stress on the values of independence and strength also leads American corporations to make profits rather than market share the key to their security. As a result, American corporations practice self-restraint of a variety not seen in Japan. Cut-throat competition is avoided, as are excessively high levels of investment that may prove unprofitable in the long run by creating overcapacity. Finally, the compulsion to remain independent and strong explains the refusal of American corporations to "die," or in any case to contract, even after they enter the senescent state - as well as their readiness to invoke the protectionist alternative.

On the other hand, the sense of helplessness means that Japanese corporations feel a compulsion to take maximum advantage of short-run opportunities to carve out a large share of the market for themselves through high levels of investment and cut-throat competition. As a result, it is not uncommon to find selling prices dropping below the average cost of production in an industry, with obvious severe consequences for the less efficient producers. In Japan, the helplessness mentality does result in protectionist demands, but not in the senescent stage of industrial development. The heightened Japanese sense of vulnerability is reflected in the fact that industries seek protection during their infant stage and even beyond that stage, when it is no longer necessary. However, when Japanese industries reach the senescent stage, they accept their fate relatively easily. This social psychology is also reflected in the way in which people view their national economy. Japanese tend to think theirs is more vulnerable than it really is; Americans tend to think theirs is stronger than it actually is.

Another factor that has contributed to the dynamism of the Japanese industrial structure is the high quality of the labor force, founded on a very strong work ethic. Social scientists have described the work ethic in the United States as a combination of individualism and activism derived from the Protestant ethic. The Japanese work ethic is actually a different attitude altogether, one that has been closely linked to a family-type collectivism. Every social group maintains its cohesion by means of a commonly shared goal. In Japan, at least until recently, that goal has been the universal desire of the Japanese people to match and surpass the achievements of the West. Individual and group efforts directed toward that goal are identified with the public interest, and, therefore, hard work, self-restraint, and a propensity to save rather than spend are regarded as patriotic patterns of behavior.

The Japanese work ethic, then, is not based significantly on the desire for individual recognition. Rather it is based on a success-seeking urge whose goals and rewards are defined collectively. For the Japanese, individual behavior is evaluated in terms of its benefit to the society as a whole. At the same time, social pressures for conformity are very strong in Japan. The Japanese intolerance of nonconformism - an expression of the intense desire to preserve the homogeneity and distinctive identity of Japanese society - means that the dropout cannot easily survive. Finally, the individual's work ethic is reinforced by the widespread belief in the possibility of upward social mobility. Consequently, the individual works hard to be promoted within the organization. Only in this last respect does the work ethic in Japan parallel the one that operates in the United States.

Demographic changes in the Japanese labor force are unlikely to produce any significant changes in industrial structure in Japan. It is true that the average age of the Japanese population will surpass that of the United States in 1985, after which the U.S. average will decline while that of Japan will continue to increase. However, this trend does not necessarily entail a decline in productivity in Japan. One necessary step for avoiding a reduction in Japanese labor productivity will be to adjust the system of seniority-linked automatic wage increases to accord with the changed demographic structure. (This will not involve any modification in the system of lifetime employment.) Increased investment in human capital can also improve the quality of labor. Moreover, the shift in industrial structure toward more knowledge-intensive industries will expand the opportunities for utilizing older people's knowledge and experience. The real problem of the elderly society is the aging of leadership, with a consequent decline in the energy and imagination of leaders in facing the challenges of the future.(1)

In conclusion, I think that the analysis of industrial structure in the United States and Japan sheds light on the significance of two events which occurred during the negotiations between our two countries. The first was a message from the United States urging Japan to promote the efficiency of its economy by opening its market in those inefficient sectors where the market has been closed for social and political reasons. The second was a message from the Japanese side to the United States urging that measures be taken to promote the reorganization of the U.S. industrial structure in order to improve its international competitiveness. It appears, then, that our recent economic disputes have not been without their constructive aspects. It is to be hoped that each side interprets the other's message not as a challenge based on bad faith, but as a useful and earnest suggestion. In that case, a solid basis for the development of truly cooperative and friendly relations will have been established.

NOTES

1. For a different point of view, see the comments of Peter
    F. Drucker, in "Japan: the Problems of Success," <u>Foreign
    Affairs</u>, April 1978, pp. 564-578.

7 Japanese Corporate Behavior: An Outside View

Benjamin M. Rowland

What animates a Japanese corporation? Is it profit, or survival as an entity? Is it service to some higher ideal by which it can even accept its own death with equanimity? The West understands well enough the first two notions. It also understands, at least in theory, the idea of corporate aging and death. Textbooks abound with descriptions of the "product cycle theory" in which industries are born in advanced centers and then migrate to less costly regions as the advantages of technology cease to offset the advantages of lower factor costs. Indeed, the West is the author of the Code of Liberal Conduct under which the strong are meant to prosper and the weak perish according to the rules of the game. In the West, then, the final arbiter of corporate success or failure is meant to be the impersonal marketplace. In Japan, however, although corporate success may happen to coincide (indeed, most frequently does coincide) with market success, the marketplace is not meant to be the determining factor. For in Japan, corporations are said to serve a larger plan which is more a style of life than it is a particular strategy.

The vulnerability of that lifestyle and the seeming inability of Japanese institutions to develop a new consensus to preserve it are the very broad questions that underlie this analysis of corporate behavior in Japan. Since the Meiji Restoration, Japan has been held up as the model of a country that adopted a Western economy without becoming a Western society. But increasing international hostility and a deepening recession at home have been eroding the devices by which Japan has traditionally kept the West at bay. Corporations in Japan have been the chief instrumentality for achieving that balance - for blending competition with a style of social paternalism unique to Japan. It is a marriage of talents that seems increasingly unsustainable. Put very crudely, Japanese corporations face the choice of shedding their social baggage or demanding of the state an environment in which this baggage can continue to be carried. It is not clear yet which way the Japanese will go, but the consequences of either prospect for Japanese corporate behavior will be profound.

As an outsider viewing Japanese corporate behavior, I find the "Japan, Inc." myth useful, even in the knowledge that this is a highly imperfect description of how Japanese enterprise really functions. True or not, it is a persisting ideal or "idea force" in Japan, like the "free trade" or "free enterprise" myths in the United States. Deviations cause dissonance, confusion, and national discomfort. As more than one observer has noted, the Japanese spirit yearns for the final unanimous decision. The impulse for consensus is strong.

Consensus building in Japan is often said to flow from Japan's strong cultural tradition of paternalism and its uniquely homogeneous population - in short, from Japan as a nation. But Japan is also a state, a disciplinary apparatus that punishes and rewards its many interest groups in order to achieve goals that are social and political as well as narrowly economic. Yet if one assumes that the desire for conformity is no less strong today than in the past, the means at the disposal of the state and the incentives available to corporations for achieving that end would appear to be in increasingly scarce supply. At present, Japanese corporations (and their mentor, the state) confront an unusually harsh set of circumstances. Trading partners no longer welcome the outpouring of goods which enabled Japan to lift itself out of earlier recessions. They clamor for greater access to Japan's internal markets at a time when high unemployment and overcapacity in basic industry are immense problems in themselves. The strong currency punishes some companies even as it rewards others, making compromise more difficult. Finally, the ability of the state to foster an orderly transition from nonviable to viable industries, or to promote general reflation, is also approaching its limits, as least as the system is presently constituted. Government debt currently represents well over one-third of government expenditure. Finding new holders for that debt seems to raise nearly as many problems as it solves.

Let me return again to the notion of Japan Inc., that mutual benefit society of individuals, banks, enterprise, and the state, in order to bring some of its present stress points into better relief. In the years of recovery and high growth, when corporations were unable to generate sufficient internal cash, banks lent their money unstintingly while relying on liberal overdraft facilities from the Bank of Japan when loans exceeded deposits. The banks in turn submitted themselves to

minute government scrutiny, endured an environment of
dictated interest rates, and agreed to accept in their portfolios
the vast majority of government indebtedness.

High levels of lending drew the banks ever closer to their
principal corporate borrowers, and interlocking directorships
and crossholding of shares became the rule of the day - a
practice which had strong precedents in prewar Japan. Major
corporations did not go bankrupt; banks carried them until
they were whole again, but in doing so, they could count on
special consideration from the Bank of Japan in the form of
free deposits or other devices. The strong companies helped
the weak, at least indirectly, by borrowing heavily whether
they really needed the money or not. Individuals served
loyally and were rewarded with job security. They placed
their extensive savings overwhelmingly in bank time deposits
which returned again as further loans to the corporations.

The many problems in this system have received wide
attention, not least from the Japanese themselves. As an
outsider, however, I sense that their cumulative impact, if
anything, has been understated. Let me focus on three of
them - unemployment, the "structural recession," and the
related problems of financing recovery - to illustrate my point.

The unemployment problem in Japan touches directly on
the question of the lifestyle which corporations in the past
have so successfully preserved. Lifetime employment, of
course, has never been a universal feature of Japanese
corporate life. By one estimate, it has never encompassed
more than 35 percent of the working population. But its role
as an ideal standard and as an instrument of social cohesion
seems beyond dispute. Edwin Reischauer's description of the
system is particularly good:

> Those higher on the career escalator are seen as
> merely older persons who got on the escalator earlier,
> not as persons who have scrambled unfairly to the
> top. One's own time will come in due course. Or if
> they are on a superior escalator to one's own, this
> is because of their superior achievements in education
> and examinations . . .the result of differences in
> personal ability, not of an unfair society. The lack
> of dictatorial authority on the part of the leaders and
> the wide consultations and sharing of decision making
> powers tend to make a subordinate's position less
> irksome than in the West. The close solidarity of the
> Group, the lingering sense of paternalistic concern
> on the part of those on top, and the personal loyalty
> on the part of those below give a feeling of warmth
> and intimacy across status lines. And finally the
> sense of belonging - of achieving a sense of self-
> identity through membership in a group - makes the

individual more willing to accept his status, whatever it may be.(1)

The unemployment problem has two related dimensions: the pressure of excess workers today, and the prospect of an aging labor force implying higher labor costs for the future (see Table 7.1). Current official unemployment hovers at around 2.3 percent – a figure far lower than would be the case if American measures were used. If Japan's employed but redundant workers – estimated at between two and three million – were discharged into the marketplace, the rate of unemployment would climb to perhaps 6.5 percent. The costs to industry in carrying them are self-evident. Custom also dictates that wage rates are linked to seniority, meaning that labor costs automatically increase over time unless offset by productivity gains or by the introduction of enough cheap labor at the base of the pay scale to distribute the overall burden. The latter strategy, of course, assumes the availability of youthful labor and future rapid growth, neither of which seems likely.

Increasingly, the employment problem is forcing corporations to make a difficult choice between their social roles and their economic roles. A Ministry of International Trade and Industry (MITI) survey of 303 major manufacturers released in November 1978 disclosed that half the respondents had surplus employees, averaging around 13 percent of the total employed; 46 percent intended to reduce their work force over the near and medium term. Dismissal by one's "lifetime employer," to be sure, does not necessarily mean either unemployment or a total absence of compensation. Corporations make great efforts to place their redundant workers with other enterprises. Those not placed are bought off with generous pensions. But the ability of the economy to absorb excess labor is limited as is the ability of weakened companies to provide pensions.

Unfortunately, the problem is exacerbated further by the vast differences in efficiency between the "secondary sector" on the one hand, and the "primary" and "tertiary" sectors on the other. Ordinarily, one would expect that as market forces reduced the rate of return in the traditional industry sector, resources would then flow into alternative uses. But the "gradient" between productivity in manufacturing and productivity in other sectors is so steep that the result would almost certainly be higher, not lower, unemployment. Even if the political and institutional barriers to reform could be lifted, major new investment in the primary and tertiary sectors could only add unacceptably large numbers of farmers and shopkeepers to the ranks of the unemployed.(2)

Public statements of corporations obliged to lay off workers or to alter lifetime employment patterns represent an

Table 7.1. Composition of Japanese Labor Force by Age

AGE BRACKET	PERCENTAGE OF WORK FORCE IN EACH AGE BRACKET FROM 1965 TO 1990			Projected 1990
	1965	1970	1975	
15-19 years	9.8	6.5	3.4	2.2
20-29 years	37.0	35.9	32.2	22.3
30-39 years	27.6	28.0	30.3	24.8
40-49 years	14.9	18.0	21.2	27.1
50-59 years	8.2	8.5	10.0	18.5
Over 60 years	2.5	3.0	3.0	5.1

SOURCE: Japan Economic Journal, February 14, 1978.

awkward attempt to make a social virtue out of an economic necessity. One company offered two reasons for reducing its retirement age from fifty-five to forty-five: "One, of course, is to give workers a second chance to make their own decisions for life. The other is to remind them of the importance of . . . serious soul-searching at forty-five in the face of the latter half of their careers."(3)   Another, announcing a "no mercy" merit-based wage system starting at age thirty-five, was more blunt: "If we keep the seniority wage system intact in spite of this development we will bust in about five years."(4)

It is possible to argue, of course, that many real, broadly based advantages would flow from discontinuing the policy of tenured employment. Corporate productivity would be enhanced. Presumably, the drive to export would be somewhat tempered. If wages and salaries in general could be treated as variable rather than fixed costs, the pressure to produce under any and all circumstances would be far less. And the social welfare function would no longer be lodged in industry but in government where, as some would argue, it belongs.   A further argument holds that lifetime employment is the chief culprit for widely acknowledged flaws in the Japanese educational system.   Jockeying for position to enter the best university - from which one can choose the best lifetime job - begins in early childhood and culminates in a university entry "exam hell" which by all accounts fully merits the description. Labor mobility, it is said, would remove pressure all the way down the line and transform Japanese education into a far more humane institution.

For corporations in Japan, lifetime employment is an increasingly onerous, perhaps unsustainable responsibility. But it seems plausible to argue, in a broad sense, that that responsibility has given rise to certain privileges as well.   As an outsider, for example, I find it hard to separate the lifetime employment practice from the widespread tolerance for cartels.

Traditionally, resistance in Japan to cartels, orderly marketing procedures, and the network of business relationships which underlie them has been slight. By common consent, the Japanese shrugged off America's attempt to impose its own antitrust regulations on Japan almost as soon as the occupying forces had departed. But it is probably more than coincidence that a revival of interest in the antimonopoly laws should have appeared during the present recession. To be sure, the revised laws in their final form are hardly proof that the present system is in imminent danger: ambitious proposals for change have been watered down or eliminated, and the only surviving law of substance requires companies to reduce their cross-holding of shares from 10 percent to 5 percent over a leisurely ten-year period.   Nevertheless, the renewed interest in antitrust legislation in Japan bespeaks a certain loss of ease with the cartel system.   Few people will quarrel with a cartel if they are included within its protective circle.   Higher costs are tolerable if you still have a job.   But would a new constituency of the unemployed view industry's cartels and exclusionary practices with the same indifference from the outside?   Probably not.   And unemployment is only one of the very complex problems Japanese corporations face in the months and years ahead.   If Japan chooses to solve its present difficulties by removing one set of interests from the consensual group, the legitimacy of the remaining interests must fall under increasingly skeptical scrutiny.

In the past, the principles of consensus and social cohesion are said to have applied as much to relations among corporations as within them.   In an economic downturn, the keen competition that normally characterizes Japanese corporate behavior is placed to some degree in suspension.   Cooperative measures prevail so that all may survive.   Today those measures are complicated, among other reasons, by the depth of the present recession and the extraordinary strength of the yen.

Broad outlines of what might be a consensus plan have been advanced by many parties.   They show a certain degree of unanimity. All agree, for example, that Japan must shift its industrial structure toward higher value-added production.   Of course there is nothing new in that suggestion; it has been a staple of Japanese planning since the early 1960s, if not before.   The desirability of developing "knowledge-intensive industry" is another common, if somewhat vague, feature.   But few seem prepared to state that such activities are adequate in themselves to become the engine of another Japanese growth era.

The gravest problem of all is the disposal of the chronically ill "traditional" sectors of industry that provided the impetus for growth in the past.   One economist has divided the sick industry sectors of the Japanese economy into three major groupings: 1) those suffering from excess capacity, but expected to return to health in the next economic upturn, for example, steel, shipping, shipbuilding; 2) those not expected to regain their former vitality because of higher energy costs, for example, aluminum smelting, chemical fertilizers, and synthetic fibers; and 3) those sectors, such as textiles, plywood, and others, where the advantage has irrevocably passed to developing countries with lower costs.(5)

Implied, of course, is the assumption that those which can recover should be nurtured, and those which cannot, abandoned.   The problem lies not in the vision, which seems reasonable enough, but in the execution.   The fact is that corporations resist death no less in Japan than in the United States.   To take one example, in the spring and summer of

1978, Japanese textile lobbyists launched an energetic attack against the automobile and high-technology sectors, arguing that "export dumping" by these industries was the chief reason for the appreciation of the yen. Forcing exports, they continued, was an "antisocial" activity because driving up the yen rate made competition abroad impossible for weaker economic sectors. Joined by other weak industry groups, the textile interests lobbied the government for voluntary export controls. Their goals, to be sure, were shared by many industries abroad. I suspect, however, that these internal efforts had a large impact on the final successful outcome.

Enforcing these voluntary controls has been a different matter. For example, one major automobile company announced in the spring of 1978 that it had no intention of observing the controls. In any event, the pattern of exports in the intervening months does little to support the view that the program has been a success.

Still, the historical evidence is strong that Japan has been more successful at making major structural adjustments than its Western counterparts. Why shouldn't it be equally successful this time around? The answer, I believe, lies in the fact that the state has relatively few financial resources at its disposal today to effect the transition. The financial marketplace is much more narrowly based in Japan than, for example, in the United States. A small handful of financial institutions - chiefly banks and insurance companies - own most of the equity and nearly all of the debt of corporate Japan. By comparison, the habit of risk taking by private individuals is very limited. In the past, the national and municipal governments financed their relatively modest deficits by making compulsory placements with the banks and other financial institutions. There was slight risk in accumulating this debt because interest rates were dictated and held relatively constant by the government itself. With the recent massive government bond issues, the absorptive capacity of this narrow financial system is widely seen to be approaching its limits. In the spring of 1979, banks and securities companies actually boycotted a government debt offering because rates were too low - a perhaps unprecedented act of defiance against official authorities. But the principal victim of the higher rates that followed will certainly be corporate Japan itself, with its high degree of dependence on borrowed money. For as rates move higher, corporate debt repayments will also increase, and corporations may again resort to the unwelcome strategy of forcing exports abroad to cover higher costs.

Implicitly, if not explicitly, the key to Japan's economic and financial system, and the touchstone of the "Japan, Inc." myth as well, has been the premise that the state will serve as the risk taker of last resort. In times of difficulty in the past, corporations could turn to banks, and banks to the state, to weather economic turbulence. The recent recession, however, and the prospect of further difficulties ahead have proven that the state's resources are not inexhaustible. The state itself - its ability to cajole, coax, and mandate change - is in danger of falling victim to the risk-averse environment it has created.

In summary, given the current recession and the growing inability of the state to shield the economy from its impact, corporate behavior will become increasingly independent and responsive to market forces. As corporations are forced to abandon their traditional roles as providers of social welfare, their own privileges will be called into question more and more. Competition will become keener. Faction will predominate over cooperation. At some juncture, if the distance between the old consensual state and the emerging order of things grows too great, it is not impossible to imagine state intervention to recreate conditions in which consensus might operate once again. That, in turn, would imply a more closed and nationalistic Japan, with consequences reaching well beyond the scope of this essay.

To be sure, there is a more optimistic view as well. One can reasonably argue that Japan has progressed too far ever to revert to insularity; the consequences - economic, social, and political - of such a reversion would be unimaginable. And if a continued commitment to internationalism will mean the loss of consensus, Japan may well be willing to pay this price. The consensual system served a specific historical purpose: the resurrection of Japan from the ashes of World War II. This function completed, it should be possible for Japan to abandon the consensual system pragmatically and unsentimentally.

Japan is justly famous for its ability to solve intractable problems. In the coming years, this ability will be fully tested.

NOTES

(1) Edwin O. Reischauer, The Japanese (Cambridge, Mass.: Harvard University Press, 1977), p. 166.

(2) See Brian Reading, "Efficiency of Japanese is not true - it happens to be 'myth'," in Japan Economic Journal Supplement, April 11, 1978, pp. 23-24.

(3) Japan Economic Journal, April 18, 1978, p. 20.

(4) Japan Economic Journal, May 9, 1978, p. 20.

(5) Takayuki Hazumi, "Outlook of Japanese Economy under International Pressure and Appreciating Currency" (Unpublished paper delivered in London, October 8, 1977).

8 Government-Business Relations in Japan and the United States: A Study in Contrasts

Kiichi Mochizuki

In the August 28, 1978 issue of the New Yorker, economist Robert Heilbroner declares that we are on the verge of a new era in economic history, one which he characterizes as "planned capitalism." This change is taking place largely in response to our increasing awareness of such environmental constraints as pollution and the energy shortage. Within this context, Heilbroner argues, only a high degree of economic planning, supported by extensive institutional change, will be able to rescue the capitalist system. He notes that the skeleton of such a planning effort already exists in the United States in the various agencies and authorities scattered throughout the federal bureaucracy.

It is true that both the United States and Japan, as advanced industrial societies, have already started down the road of planned or state capitalism. However, the Japanese system is better suited to the gradual increase in government involvement in the private sector which Heilbroner foresees. Where America profited in the past by allowing its business interests as much freedom as possible to extract whatever they wanted from an environment overflowing with resources, the Japanese have always found it necessary to coordinate their economic efforts in order to support a large population on a meagre landscape. Also, the Japanese system is more pragmatic than the American: it is not constrained by devotion to any principle other than that of its own survival, while the American economy is hobbled by its reverence for the free enterprise system and its anxiety over government interference in the marketplace. More important, the Japanese corporation, as part of a society structured by vertical clusters, is more congenial to the development of state capitalism, since these clusters provide built-in series of connections between the public and private sectors.

Ironically, however, while the American system has been reluctantly moving more and more toward the interpenetration of public and private sectors, the long-existing Japanese mechanism for such coordination has become a stagnating element, insulating the vertical clusters against external stimuli.

In the following pages, I will discuss the historical and social background of the relationship between government and business in both Japan and the United States, concentrating upon the differences in their respective corporate structures and the impact of these differences upon each economy's adaptability to the participation of government in the private sector.

The identity of an American corporation is ultimately represented by the value of its stock. U.S. corporations function as single individuals whose self-interest is expressed in terms of the profit motive. On the other hand, the Japanese corporation is a social entity with multiple functions and goals, a sort of cross-section of Japanese society. The difference between the identities of Japanese and American corporations can be clearly seen in the contrasting functions of the stockholders' meetings for each. In American corporations, stockholders play important roles in influencing corporate management, since they are the cells of the organism, and the chairman of the board of an American corporation is more powerful than the corporation president. By contrast, Japanese stockholders are barely more than investors who have little to do with the management of the business, and the chairman of the board is frequently only a retired corporation president. While the only external check on the activities of American corporations is the regulation of the Federal Securities and Exchange Commission, Japanese corporations, as social entities with multiple functions, are held accountable to numerous elements in Japanese society - bankers, government officials, labor leaders, consumers, and other members of the general public who have nothing to do with the ownership of the corporation. This sort of accountability is only beginning to develop in the United States, and such is the freedom of the American corporation that this accountability must be expressed in terms of specific legal constraints. In Japan, however, the pressure on the corporation to respect the public interest is societal rather than legal, implicit rather than explicit. As an individual driven chiefly by the simply determined profit motive, and checked only by the minimal restraints of the government, the American corporation is much freer to move than its Japanese counterpart, whose policies are evolved very slowly and deliberately through a process of consensus. The Japanese corporation is capable of moving very decisively once a consensus has been established, but, in the absence of a clear consensus, there is no energetic pursuit of a corporate direction and no explicit debate in search of one. Hence the Japanese corporation is characterized in its day-to-day dealings by very slow changes in management, with a complex decision-making process and an emphasis upon reputation at the expense of solid business results.

Westerners often point to lifetime employment, the seniority system, and consensual decision making as the distinguishing features of the Japanese corporate system. In actuality, these characteristics are far from universal in Japanese industry, and all of them appear, in one form or another, in the American system as well. However, these features are manifestations of the fact that Japanese industry - and Japanese society as well - is constructed around a system of vertical clusters, and it is this structure which is the distinguishing feature of the Japanese economy.

Japanese society developed vertical clusters as a result of the early national unification of Japan in the seventh century. The establishment of a central government so early on enabled Japan to entertain vertical divisions of the nation without fear of national disintegration. In modern Japan, a major cluster includes corporations involved in a particular industrial sector, along with the government agency responsible for that sector and politicians with interests in the area. Smaller clusters within this major unit consist of the business contacts, subcontractors, suppliers, and customers of individual corporations. Although these networks can be insecure at the periphery, the central clusters are quite firmly entrenched. It is very difficult to move from one cluster to another, since one is likely to sacrifice the guarantee of lifetime employment in the process, and advancement must proceed internally, by means of the seniority system. Since the composition of the cluster is therefore quite stable, relationships among the constituents must be maintained over the long term. Confrontation must be avoided and consensus is of supreme importance.

The fact that corporations are organized into this system of clusters obviously has a great impact upon the conduct of business in Japan. The bankruptcy of a corporation means the disintegration of its constituent elements, and, rather than face a bankruptcy, employees will endure a great deal in order to enable their corporation to survive. Because of the emphasis upon consensus, confrontations and radical departures from an established policy rarely occur. Clusters are very dependent upon the establishment of goals as a means of mobilizing their various constituents. Once the goal has been accomplished, the cluster loses its direction, and its efficiency suffers. This helps to account for the fact that Japanese factories - whose goals are very easily defined in production terms - operate much more efficiently than any other aspect of the Japanese economy, where goal setting is more difficult.

The absence of confrontation inside the cluster organization results not only in belated goal setting and decision making, but also in the stagnation of the management, because there is little external pressure for managerial innovation.

In the late 1970s, the efficiency of the core clusters appears to be diminishing. Cluster goals are no longer being generated, and the compensation for cluster loyalty, the system of lifetime employment, appears to have been shaken by the long recession. If the present cluster system does lose its grip, as seems likely, the Japanese economy will become stagnant, and these conditions will prevail until a new national goal revitalizes the system and the clusters are rejuvenated by an infusion of new leadership.

Let me develop in greater detail the structural features that distinguish the relationship between public and private sectors in Japan. Japan's administrative bureaucracy is organized in such a way that the ministries and bureaus correspond to particular industries, with the exception of several functional ministries. Labor unions, corporations, industries, and their corresponding ministry in one business area together form a sectoral vertical cluster. Japanese legislators do not necessarily work for their respective geographic districts, but rather tend to represent interests that might be based in various regions of the country. Thus legislators from different areas of Japan are likely to bond together in their representation of a particular industrial cluster, themselves becoming part of that structure. One of the principal advantages of this system is the fact that it greatly facilitates communication between the government and the business community.

This structure arose in the nineteenth century in Japan because local interests had become relatively weak after a long history of national unity, and the national government took upon itself the task of promoting industrial development in the face of foreign economic invasions. By contrast, the U.S. federal government was created to defend already established local governments and businesses from foreign intervention. American industries have historically kept their contact with the federal government to a minimum. Communications between business and government are most often conducted through the channel of Congressional lobbying, which tends to pick up local, short-term, and emotional issues without fitting them into the entire spectrum of competing interests and without relating them to the general good of the nation. In Japan, legislators must filter their sectoral interests through a national bureaucracy intended to safeguard the national interest. Thus political extremes are modulated and consistent policies emerge.

This description represents the Japanese system at its best. However, it must be understood that this system has undergone an evolution as a result of various historical circumstances, and, as mentioned above, it appears to have entered a period of decline in the late 1970s. Historically, at the time of the Meiji Revolution in 1868, when the Japanese government initiated its drive for industrial development, the more highly educated and motivated individuals entered government service, while the caliber of people working in industry was generally inferior. Young and ambitious men were drawn to the revolutionary government, inflamed by the aspiration to push their nation to the forefront of the world through both industrial and military development. During the early 1900s, the private sector began to attract a greater share of talented people, and Japanese business became somewhat more independent of government influence as a result of the wealth accumulated during the Sino-Japanese War, the Russo-Japanese War, and World War I. Soon after, however, the advent of the Great Depression brought on a series of trade disputes which led to the disintegration of the world economy into blocs, and Japan was cut off from its supply of crude oil. In order to obtain resources from overseas and allocate them appropriately, Japan strengthened the coordination of industrial and government activities by instituting a centrally planned and regulated economy. And after World War II, the reconstruction of Japan's war-destroyed industrial sectors only increased the need for cooperation between government and business.

By 1970, however, most of Japan's industries had been firmly established. The "infant industry" type of protection by the Ministry of International Trade and Industry was abolished by this time, and the industrial clusters linked to it for the purpose of industrial development began to fade away. The Japanese export industries have been exposed to strong international stimuli through their export activities. However, other industry clusters unrelated to MITI - for example, those associated with the Ministries of Finance, Agriculture, Construction, Transportation, and Education - have not benefited from the influence of such foreign input, and have therefore become insular and parochial. Government-business relations in these areas must be reviewed in the light of Japan's increasing involvement in the international scene and in the light of changing world conditions. Relations that once served the national interest may no longer fulfill Japan's needs. The fact that the cluster structure itself tends to promote complacency and stagnation represents an obstacle to the reform of the present Japanese system. The Japanese have come a long way in terms of government-business interaction since the Meiji Revolution, but the Japanese system has, for the first time, begun to lose its sense of purpose, and confusion may prevail for a long time to come.

In the case of the United States, of course, the social background of the corporate structure is entirely different, based upon the functional participation of individuals who are freer to move from organization to organization. A vertically organized social structure like that of Japan requires a deeply entrenched national government and was therefore not possible throughout much of the relatively brief history of the United States. Instead, because of the vastness of the American territory, geographical subdivisions, rather than vertical divisions, have been the rule. However, just as the system of vertical clusters appears to be loosening in Japan in the late 1970s, so the United States now appears to be developing its own set of sectoral clusters, with the rise of special interest groups and single-issue politics and the growing responsiveness of American politicians to the lobbying efforts of individual sectors.

This development represents quite a change for the American system, which has, throughout its history, vigorously resisted the linkage of public and private sectors. The patterns of government interventions are by now well established in most economies throughout the world, appearing in developed and developing nations alike. And yet the United States has stood out as a peculiarly vocal advocate of the free enterprise system.

The American reverence for the free enterprise system - unique in the world - might be explained in several ways. First of all, the United States is a nation originally made up of the victims of various kinds of persecutions and institutional constraints, and this historical circumstance might help to account for the traditional American assertion of the individual's freedom over the state's sovereignty. Second, the national unification of the United States occurred after businesses were established on its shores. Indeed, a very important impetus of the American Revolution and the establishment of an independent American government was the protection of local business from the control of the British government. In this sense, the United States is virtually unique among the advanced industrial powers, most of which began, not as colonies, but as sovereign states. As noted above, Japan's own national government dates from the seventh century, and it has survived numerous changes in its economic system. Although one might argue that governments in several of the industrial nations have themselves been overthrown and replaced, what is important here is the fact that the existence of a national government, regardless of its form, has itself never been questioned. In fact, several of the governments of the latecomer capitalist nations - for example, Japan and Germany - actually took it upon themselves to promote the industrialization of their countries in order to defend them against the economic incursions of the early starters among the capitalist powers. The prerevolutionary government of nineteenth-century Japan was inflicted with an unequal duty treaty by the United States and only recovered its sovereignty on the duty after a struggle of twenty years. Therefore, government and business in Japan grew together, cooperating for the welfare of the nation. The fact that regional authorities in the United States, in the form of the various state governments, have been guaranteed a certain level of individual autonomy also helps to account for American uneasiness over Washington's interference in business affairs. Most American businesses spent their formative years within the boundaries of the states in which they were established, enjoying locally tailored government-business relations. Their expansion beyond state borders has brought them into contact with federal interstate commerce regulations, an interaction they have by and large resented. This holds true even in recent years, as the regional power of the Sun Belt has encouraged the vociferous denunciation of federal regulations on the part of business interests in California and Texas.

Of course, the American resistance to government intervention is by no means universally applicable. Often American industry seeks, and benefits from, governmental interference. Yet it is silent about such instances and raises its voice only to protest the application of regulations that do not increase its profits. It is therefore important to keep in mind the fact that there exist fairly strong precedents for the coordination of public and private sectors in the United States. The federal government has been actively involved in the American business sector since the time of the New Deal, when the Tennessee Valley Authority was launched by Washington to stimulate employment and revitalize the economy. Basic industries developed by the government during World War II were transferred to private ownership after the war. And one of the major denominators of American diplomacy has been the promotion of the American extractive industries abroad. Numerous examples of such activities include the involvement of the State Department and the American oil industry in the Iranian Consortium during the Mossadeque coup, the establishment of American refineries in Japan and West Germany under the postwar American occupation, and the recent CIA involvement in the Chilean copper industry. The Defense Department, by promoting research and development and nurturing infant industries in the areas of weaponry, aircraft, and electronics, has played an essential role as an architect of the present-day American economy. The munitions, aircraft, and computer industries are the very sectors in which the United States currently enjoys a world-wide competitive advantage, and there is no question that these industries owe their development to Defense Department contracts.

This is plentiful evidence of government-business coordination throughout the current American economy. The Treasury Department and the International Trade Commission protect declining American industries through import regulations and adjustment assistance. Programs of assistance and subsidy have been established to aid particular sectors of American industry - for example, steel and shipbuilding - and Congress has formed a large steel caucus. Many state governments have enacted "Buy American" legislation. And the U.S. government has become the major promoter of international business coordinating mechanisms, such as the Multilateral Fiber Agreement, the International Energy Agency, and the International Steel Committee. It is therefore impossible to claim that American industry has grown without governmental assistance. And the cooperation between public and private sectors appears to be growing increasingly ex- plicit. Already several "Industry Sector Advisory Committees" have been established to coordinate the activities of govern- ment, business, and labor. Thus, although they are not as conspicuous as the more institutionalized Japanese clusters, if all the separate pieces of government involvement in American industry were studied and classified by industrial sector, it would be possible to observe the gradual buildup of a system of vertical clusters in the United States over the years since the Great Depression.

It has been proposed that, since the oil crisis of 1973, the developed nations have entered a new stage in the history of capitalism. The earliest form of capitalism consisted of the crude, nineteenth-century brand of competition and free enterprise. The next stage, the era of big business, occurred around the turn of the century, while the third stage - just concluded - was marked by the increased involvement of government in the private sector between the Great Depression and the early 1970s. In the fourth stage of capitalism - born as a result of the energy crisis - the government sector will actively cooperate with private enterprise in order to coordinate market forces both domestically and internationally. In this era of state capitalism, corporations and governments will be forced to become structurally involved in each other through clusters of sectoral interests.

I have argued that Japanese corporations are better prepared for this situation, since they already exist as social organisms within a system of vertical clusters that institutionalize cooperation between government and business. But such clusters tend to reject external influences, and this absence of external stimulation may unfortunately lead to the stagnation of many portions of the Japanese system. In the areas where export requirements expose the clusters to external forces, Japanese corporations will maintain their efficiency. However, in the areas in which external input is confined to imports and foreign investment - such as agriculture, distribution, finance, weaponry, and education - Japan's industries may deteriorate because of their structural insulation.

American corporations have further to go than their Japanese counterparts to adjust themselves to the requirements of state capitalism. These corporations have pursued their own interests as individuals throughout most of their history, and the U.S. government has by and large minimized its sovereignty over these individuals. Ironically American businesses, such vocal advocates of the virtues of free competition, welcome the interference of the government in the free enterprise system when they can no longer compete successfully. The purely financial approach of American corporations has begun in recent years to yield to the social demand that the corporation be recognized as an entity whose activities vitally affect many people. As a result, vertical clusters appear to be emerging in the relationship between the American government and business community through the growing phenomenon of single-issue politics and the clamor for sectoral assistance. Where the Japanese system, by institutionalizing the government-business relationship, has managed to shape the various sectoral interests into consistent policies that serve the social interest, the American system is not yet sufficiently coordinated to balance the competing claims of individual special interests into a national policy. In this sense, the American adherence to the rhetoric of free enterprise may impede the development of institutions effectively linking the public and private sectors into a consistently functioning whole.

In sum, Japan is more fitted structurally to the onset of state capitalism. The system of vertical clusters it developed in order to nurture Japanese industry has done its job well, but may result in its own stagnation. The free American system may have worked well in the past, but it is now prone to being tyrannized by individual concerns. Also, the fundamental American belief in the primacy of individual freedom over all other values runs directly counter to the social orientation that underlies state capitalism. It is possible that both systems will manage to adapt themselves to the requirements of the resource-poor, global capitalism of the future. It is also possible that both will fail, defeated by the very factors that enabled each to flourish throughout earlier phases of capitalism.

III

Sources of Cooperation in U.S.—Japanese Relations: Policy Recommendations

9 Convergence or Collision: Alternative Scenarios for U.S.—Japanese Relations

Kenichi Imai

Although it is necessary to deepen our understanding of past behaviors and their roots, we must, at this point, focus our attention upon what needs to be done in the future to improve economic relations between Japan and the United States. What sort of policy can be designed to maximize cooperation between these two countries and minimize their conflict, keeping in mind the basic differences between their respective economic structures and corporate behaviors?

To begin with, it should be noted that these differences cannot be ignored, since they lie at the heart of the economic conflicts between Japan and the United States. However, my principal concern is the point that there are several converging tendencies in the American and Japanese economies that should become more evident as time goes on, and my policy suggestions will be directed toward encouraging these convergences. I will present two extreme policy scenarios representing the best and worst possible alternatives for the future course of economic relations between Japan and the United States. According to the ideal scenario, both countries, confronted with similar problems as advanced industrial powers, will seek to reconstruct such domestic infrastructures as urban facilities, public transportation, schools, hospitals, etc. In this process, the United States will rejuvenate its obsolete industrial sector, while Japan will decentralize its economic structure and shift from an export-oriented economy to one based on domestic demand. Alternatively, according to the worst scenario, Japan will accelerate its export growth rate because of policy failures coupled with a stagnation in domestic demand. This action will invite protectionist reactions from the American side, with the general effect of exacerbating the political and economic tensions between the two countries. I will conclude with several concrete suggestions regarding the future direction of the Japanese economy, proposing a number of policy designs intended to guide Japan through its difficult transition in the next few years from a thirty-year concentration upon economic recovery to a focus upon societal reconstruction and the further improvement of the daily lives of the Japanese people.

MACROECONOMIC STRUCTURES

The chief differences between the American and Japanese macroeconomies can be broken down into four components. First, the Japanese public saves, and Japanese industries invest, a much higher percentage of their earnings than their American counterparts. Second, as a result of this high savings and investment ratio, the physical plant of Japanese industry is in considerably better condition than that of the American manufacturing sector. Third, Japan's manpower pool includes a much larger proportion of skilled industrial workers, while the United States has relatively larger pools of professional and managerial workers on the one hand, and unskilled laborers on the other. Finally, the United States enjoys an overwhelming superiority over Japan in its endowment of natural resources. All of these factors contribute to the tension between the United States and Japan, but there are signs that the gaps may be narrowing in some instances, and in any case, it happens to be in the national interest of each country to take steps to bring it into greater alignment with the other.

The Japanese personal savings ratio is extremely high in comparison with that of the United States and other developed countries, and this tendency to save is characteristic of Japanese behavior in social as well as in economic contexts. Just as Japanese people elect to limit consumer spending for future benefit, so Japanese companies are likely to expand production for the sake of future markets and invest in new plants and equipment despite the low rate of immediate return. However, it should be kept in mind that, while this high savings ratio has been one fundamental source of Japan's rapid growth, it will also become, in the long run, the primary cause of economic conflict between Japan and the rest of the world.(1) If the Japanese people continue to save rather than to spend, Japan's growth rate will continue to increase. And since this growth will be reflected in expanded production for which there is an insufficient domestic market, the Japanese share in world trade will become larger and larger, causing confrontation and conflict with other nations in a number of areas.

It cannot be expected that the Japanese savings ratio, so integral to Japan's economic growth, will decline as a result of endogenous forces in the near future, because the tendency to save is an inherent behavior of the Japanese people. However, economic forces operating outside Japan could make it impossible for Japan to maintain its high growth rate, in particular, the impending bottleneck in the availability of the world's resources. It is therefore preferable for Japan to begin to shift gradually and voluntarily to a pattern of lower economic growth in order to avoid the trauma of a sudden change. Intelligent political leadership will be necessary to guide the nation through this transition to lower growth. Obviously the government cannot order people to spend rather than save, especially in an era of resource scarcity. The alteration of such an ingrained pattern of behavior represents a fundamental problem for Japanese economic policy in the coming years; to solve it, the government must pursue a series of actions for which there exists no precedent of success in other countries. One approach would be to encourage a decline in the ratio of personal savings to income by providing enough social security and welfare benefits to alleviate people's anxiety about saving for the future. The government might also slow economic growth by making parallel investments. Later on, this essay will develop a concrete policy design that combines these two approaches. At this point, however, I want to stress the fact that, although the high rate of savings in Japanese society will inevitably continue, Japan must take measures that will ultimately lower that ratio so that it approaches that of other nations.

These short-run savings and investment patterns have greatly contributed to the efficiency of Japanese factories and equipment and thus have been critical in determining the competitive advantage of Japanese over American manufacturing industries. However, we must not overlook the simple fact that industries, like individuals, adapt themselves to their environments. American industry, from its beginnings, adopted a strategy of vertical integration because it represented the most profitable means of utilizing America's vast endowment of natural resources. Contrarily, such a strategy was not profitable for Japanese industry after World War II. Although Japan lacked natural resources at home, this need could be met abroad, since both raw materials and marine transportation were relatively inexpensive at the time. Therefore, Japanese companies used market contracts to procure resources, and concentrated at home upon reducing their manufacturing costs by increasing industrial efficiency. It was a fortunate coincidence for Japan that this investment process ran parallel to the period of postwar technological innovation.

Until the energy crisis, these corporate strategies were more appropriate to global conditions than were those of American industry. However, in the age of resource scarcity, the Japanese competitive advantage, which depended upon the availability of inexpensive raw material imports, is obviously temporary. It is highly probable that Japanese manufacturers will lose their cost advantage if they do not alter their investment strategy.

The other major source of Japan's current competitive advantage over the United States lies in the structure of its industrial labor force (see Table 9.1). The Japanese manpower pool can be classified into three levels according to its skills: the upper class - individuals with special talents in such professional fields as politics, management, academe, and art; the middle class - individuals with average knowledge and productive capacities; and the lower class - individuals who do not have the skills required for ordinary work. In comparison with the composition of the labor force in the United States, the Japanese percentage of both highly skilled and unskilled workers is relatively small, while the middle class of skilled and disciplined labor is vast. These factors have given Japanese industry a distinct advantage over its American counterpart. Where American firms employ a fairly large percentage of workers with inferior skills, Japanese industry can draw upon a wide-ranging middle class of workers who are educated, diligent, and quite responsive to corporate goals and disciplines. Although they are not necessarily creative, such individuals are the best workers in the world for the manufacturing industries.

What are the prospects for Japanese manpower in the future? Although a growing number of young workers are less receptive to company discipline, the Japanese middle class will probably retain its work ethic and high standard of labor for a while. But this advantage, like that of Japan's postwar investment strategy, will ultimately turn against Japan. The preponderance of middle level workers in Japan's manpower pool will encourage complacency with the status quo and will thus lead to the increasing rigidity of socioeconomic structures which may no longer fill Japan's needs. Correspondingly, the fact that the highly qualified, imaginative sector of the work force is small will also be felt more and more as a shortcoming, since it is this group, more than the middle sector, that possesses the talent, training, and creativity required in the reformation of Japan's social and economic systems, a task which Japan must confront in the years ahead. Just as the United States needs to raise the competency level of its less skilled workers, so Japan needs to increase the size of its managerial class. Shortages in this sector are likely to be particularly damaging in the light of increasing demand for such skills in Japan's industries over the next few years.

Table 9.1. Labor Force by Industry: Japan and the United States
(in thousands of persons and percent)

	Japan: 1970	Japan: 1975	US: 1970	US: 1975
Population	103,720	111,937	204,900	213,600
Employed	52,235	53,117	78,627	84,783
% of population	50.1	47.5	38.4	39.7
Agriculture	9,334	6,700	3,461	3,380
% of work force	17.9	12.6	4.4	4.0
Mining	216	133	515	732
	0.4	0.3	0.7	0.9
Construction	3,929	4,733	4,814	5,015
	7.5	8.9	6.1	5.9
Manufacturing	13,682	13,224	20,737	19,275
	26.2	24.9	26.4	20.6
Wholesaling	10,060	11,319	14,996	17,470
& retailing	19.3	21.3	19.1	20.6
Finance & insurance	1,104	1,384	3,942	4,665
	2.1	2.6	5.0	5.5
Services	7,635	8,690	20,266	23,759
	14.6	16.4	25.8	28.0
Government	1,720	1,963	4,473	4,770
	3.3	3.7	5.7	5.6
Fishery	535	478	NA	NA
	1.0	0.9		

SOURCE: Compiled by the Japan Trade Center.

101

Thus, although the two countries face very different problems
with respect to manpower, the competitive edge of the
Japanese labor force is likely to decline in the future.

Obviously, the disparity in natural resource endowments
is one of the most basic differences between the economies of
the United States and Japan. Because it lacks natural
resources, Japan has inevitably tended to be "mercantilist" at
least to the extent that it is always eager to accumulate
foreign reserves in order to buy resources. Japan's economic
development, its welfare and security - indeed, its very
destiny - have been completely dependent upon its ability to
procure outside resources, and its foreign economic policy has
been dictated by this urgent need.

In this age of energy shortages, it is possible that the
United States and Japan, despite the differences in their
natural endowments, will be drawn closer together by their
respective confrontations of the energy problem. The current
generation of Americans must solve the difficult tasks of
energy conservation and new energy development within its
lifetime; in the case of Japan, the development of new energy
sources represents an even more urgent problem which ought
to be recognized as a national priority. I believe that, if
Japanese energy policy takes the direction proposed below, the
resource differences between the United States and Japan will
not intensify their economic conflict but, rather, will contribute
toward their greater convergence by actually uniting them in
joint efforts based upon common needs.

CORPORATE BEHAVIORS AND MARKET ECONOMIES(2)

A number of the basic differences between the Japanese and
American economies are gradually disappearing, as symptoms of
convergence are manifesting themselves more and more. The
corporate behaviors of these two economies are usually
contrasted in terms that emphasize the individualistic
orientation and profit motive of American business on the one
hand, and the group orientation and social concerns of
Japanese business on the other. Although, of course, American industry remains highly committed to the profit motive,
the pressure of consumer groups in recent years has helped to
force U.S. industry into paying more attention to the needs of
society, and, in that process, the American business
community has begun to display the group-oriented behavior
that characterizes Japanese industry. The introduction of a
form of lifetime employment, referred to as the "new permanent
employment contract" in the American steel industry, can be
viewed as a symptom of this tendency. By way of direct
contrast, the Japanese steel industry has begun to make
increasing use of subcontract workers. In this sense, the

employment practices of these two counterpart industries are beginning to move toward each other. Similarly, although the group orientation of Japanese business is often remarked upon, it must be remembered that when Japanese firms consider alternative strategies, their ultimate deciding principle is that of long-run profit. It is true that they will take the social consequences of their actions into account, but usually only insofar as their profitability will be affected. As the recent evidence of a long recession clearly shows, if market conditions become unfavorable, companies will automatically resort to actions that assure their own survival, reverting to the profit principle regardless of the needs of society. The high growth rate of the Japanese economy has in a sense underwritten the group orientation and social consciousness of Japanese businesses in the past; the changeover to a slower growth rate will force a number of Japanese businesses to alter their practices so that they more closely correspond to the functional "American" attitudes towards profit and corporate survival.

The essential difference between the market economies of the United States and Japan lies in the degree to which these two governments control or intervene in market conduct. Since Adam Smith, the market has never been pure and free, but in the twentieth century, governments have increasingly introduced frameworks and regulations to allow the market to operate without ill effects. In general, the American system favors as little government intervention as possible; rather than directly interfering in the market, the U.S. government provides rules and frameworks designed to insure the fairness of market conduct but not to actually direct the course of market operations. In the Japanese system, government intervention in the market is much more direct and overt and may take the form of administrative guidance and investment control. The danger of such activity lies in its potential for restricting the free flow of the market and thereby making the system less responsive to dynamic economic conditions.

In Japan, this type of intervention had begun to disappear in the period between 1965 and 1975; however, recent years have seen signs of its reemergence, particularly in the areas of finance, transportation, and distribution. The reasons for expanding government involvement in the market are proliferating: the increasing openness of private business practices, the general public access to information and technology, the increase in industrial adjustment payments to ailing industries, all serve as excuses for government ministries to act upon their natural propensity to intervene in market operations. This sort of government-business relationship will not suit the future conditions of the capitalist system. Whatever we call "capitalism" from now on, the system will continue to be characterized by a high degree of fluidity and uncertainty and a need for institutional innovation. If it is to respond to these requirements, the economic system will be better served by indirect government intervention, which attempts to maximize the market's flexibility; moreover, Japan should explore new means of decentralizing its government sector. Above all, Japanese government policy should break its traditional pattern of encouraging paternalistic and group-oriented behavior.

TWO EXTREME SCENARIOS FOR UNITED STATES-JAPANESE RELATIONS

In Japan, there seems to be a vague consensus regarding the direction in which policy should be changed over the next few years. Present-day Japanese society has developed a number of urgent needs: the renewal of the large cities, the construction of new housing, health care, and educational facilities -in short, a general revitalization of the social infrastructure. At present, social welfare facilities in Japan are very poor, and the overall quality of the Japanese people's way of life is by no means commensurate with their high level of per capita income (see Table 9.2). These circumstances create tremendous demands for public investment which will necessarily produce significant repercussions in the private sector as well.

Japan must base its future economic growth upon the expansion of its domestic demand. If this expansion is successful, Japan will be able to shift its economic structure from its current dependence upon exports. Clearly Japan's export-based economic recovery has resulted in its exportation of unemployment overseas - a great source of conflict between Japan and its trading partners in this age of worldwide underemployment. An economic structure built upon domestic demand will have the double advantage of bettering daily life in Japan and, at the same time, alleviating the economic strife that has grown up between Japan and its trading partners.

On the American side, of course, the situation is not identical, since the U.S. economy is already led by domestic demand, and, as a result, the American quality of life is superior to that of Japan. Nevertheless it is apparent that the United States needs as much as Japan to encourage new investment in its domestic infrastructure. American business should decrease its private overseas spending in favor of domestic investment to restore the competitiveness of the American manufacturing sector. But the rejuvenation of American industry cannot occur unless more basic investments are made in such areas as urban renewal, mass transportation, and energy development. In this sense, both countries are

Table 9.2 Standards of Living:
Japan and the United States

	Japan	US
GNP: billions of $ ($1 = Y240)	820.5 (1978 Jan.-March)	1,995.2 (1978 Jan.-March)
Per capita income: $	5,262.5 (1978 Jan.-March)	6,215 (1978 Jan.-March)
Automobiles: persons per unit	4.86 (1975)	1.96 (1976)
Passenger cars in use per 1,000 persons	132.4 (1975)	509.9 (1976)
Park space: $10m^{(2)}$/person	1.2 (Tokyo, 1971)	19.2 (New York, 1967)
Waterwork diffusion: %	77.0 (1974)	92.9 (1967)
Sewage diffusion: %	34.7 (1974)	70.0 (1968)
Roads: total: 1,000 km	1,111.6 (1974)	6,175.3 (1975)
km/1,000 persons	10.1 (1974)	28.9 (1975)
$km/km^{(2)}$	2.9 (1974)	0.67 (1975)
paved: %	30.4 (1974)	77.6 (1975)
Housing: persons/house	4.2 (1963)	2.89 (1976)
rooms/house	4.15 (1973)	4.9 (1968)
persons/room	0.87 (1973)	0.7 (1968)

(continued)

Table 9.2.   (continued)

	Japan	US
Appliances:		
% of households with television	95.4 (1977)	99.9 (1976)
% of households with refrigerators	91.2 (1971)	99.8 (1976)
% of households with washers	93.6 (1971)	72.5 (1976)
Telephones: units/100 persons	27.1 (1975)	70.3 (1974)
Daily newspapers: copies per 1,000 persons	372.5 (1976)	283.4 (1976)
Books published: number per 1,000 persons	0.20	0.16

SOURCE: Compiled by Japan Trade Center.

confronted with similar problems in their domestic spheres; they also must both overcome tremendous obstacles within their respective economic structures to the formulation and implementation of new policy.

In the American economy, one major barrier to the development of new policy is the existence of "sector specific capital," a situation in which American corporations tend to retain too much of their earnings, thereby erecting barriers to the reallocation of capital. Nothing short of a reform of the entire tax system will be required to induce investment into the "neglected" sectors of the American economy, and the difficulties of effecting tax reform are all too familiar. Therefore, even if policy makers acknowledge the necessity to rejuvenate American industry through the leverage of public investment, various segments of the American electorate will probably offer substantial resistance to the implementation of this approach.

Similarly Japan will need to reform its old framework of capital markets if it is to generate new investment in the public sector. This problem is complicated by the fact that the long history of paternalistic government involvement in the Japanese financial sectors has contributed to the rigidity of these capital markets, making it very difficult to alter the existing flow of funds through the operation of market forces. In order to make effective public investments and at the same time prevent the bureaucratic expansion of the government, Japan should adopt various "contract" methods in cooperation with private agencies to execute public and public/private projects. This strategy would help bring about the decentralization of the government sector, although all such reforms of government procedures would, of course, require gestation periods.

According to the "best scenario" here, the economies of the United States and Japan move toward convergence in a pattern of growth led by domestic demand, as both societies concentrate their wealth upon investment in the domestic scene. There are numerous barriers and restrictions to the realization of this "best" solution in both countries. However, it is possible for each to at least move in the direction suggested by the "ideal" scenario. But before considering what steps we might take in that direction, we should review the "worst scenario" - the one that will materialize if present trends continue unchecked - in order to appreciate the urgency of the need for changing the existing patterns of government policy and corporate behavior.

If the Japanese government fails to change its policies and encourage the expansion of domestic spending, Japanese corporations will continue to orient their production toward foreign markets and the Japanese export drive will continue unchecked, further undermining Japan's economic relations

with the United States.   Actually, Japan is caught in a sort of
double bind in its trade with the United States, since Japanese
exports to American buyers will continue their accelerated
growth quite apart from the marketing efforts of Japanese
businessmen.(3)   A powerful demand for Japanese products
has developed in the United States for a number of reasons.
American consumers, with more money to spend, have come to
recognize the superior quality of goods produced in Japan,
and American businessmen have failed to respond to this
challenge as a result of their own preoccupation with
short-term profits.   Furthermore, the government protection of
some of the weaker American industries has indirectly reduced
their competitiveness by encouraging them not to mend their
ways.   Therefore, if we analyze the recent growth in Japanese
exports to the United States within the context of these
"demand pull" factors, it is possible to predict that the
importation of Japanese consumer goods into the United States
will continue to increase, even when the effect of the rising
yen is taken into account.   If the worst scenario materializes,
and Japanese business actually increases its export drive in
the face of rising costs and insufficient domestic demand, the
well-known efficiency of Japanese industry will produce and
market itself into an international nightmare: Japan will become
the manufacturing center of the world, at the cost of its
relations with its trading partners.   Aggressive exporting will
be met by aggressive protectionism, and what had once been
economic competition will become economic war.

POLICY RECOMMENDATIONS

Short of achieving the best scenario, Japan and the United
States must in any case adopt strategies that will enable them
to avoid the pitfalls of the worst scenario.   The United States
might be able to move gradually and tentatively in the
appropriate direction, since the American role is the more
passive one.   Even if the United States takes only a small step
at a time, the situation cannot help but improve somewhat.
However, the situation is quite different for Japan, the
aggressor in the worst scenario; if the Japanese government
does not actually make major policy decisions very soon to
change the present economic structure, Japanese businesses
will continue their export orientation in order to insure their
own survival.   Japan urgently needs a policy design that is
both comprehensive and practicable to guide the nation
through a very difficult phase in its socioeconomic
development.
     At this point, Japan is caught in a threefold transition -
from thirty years of rapid growth after the war, from one

hundred years of modernization, and from two hundred years as an industrial society. At such a juncture it is important to understand the logic of the change that is taking place, as well as to interpret correctly the immediate needs of the transition period itself. Japan cannot immediately hurl itself into a radical, once-for-all transformation; rather, it must reform its economic structures gradually, utilizing past capacities in the process. Japan must also confront and manage the high degree of uncertainty that necessarily accompanies a transition of such major proportions. It would be much too risky under these circumstances to settle unequivocally upon any single direction as a possible course of action. Japan must consider instead any number of alternative policies until their prospects become clear. The strategy of parallel development, well established in the field of research and development management as a means of coping with uncertainty, offers a potentially useful methodology to Japanese policy makers for experimenting with several different courses of simultaneous action during this period of transition. Above all, it is absolutely necessary that new policy be as flexible as possible and adaptable to transformation; the current system's rigidity must be reduced, not increased. The implementation of these various principles requires strong political leadership from within the Japanese government. The transition period is likely to be a difficult one, involving numerous conflicts, frictions, and dislocations; if Japan is to find its way through these, the government will have to take an active leadership role in persuading the Japanese people to accept the necessity for economic change and compensating those who may suffer from it.

I would like to propose, in the final portion of this paper, several specific policies that embody these general principles and speak to the various problems introduced above. These policies include a strategy for future investment, a new program for energy development, and a reform of the financial system, along with a concrete plan for liberalizing Japan's beef importation policy which takes into account the separate and often divergent objectives of expanding world trade, developing Japanese domestic industry, and improving the lot of the Japanese consumer.(4)

A Basic Plan for Investment in the "General Input" Sectors

During the New Deal in the 1930s, investment in hydroelectricity became a lever in the American recovery from the Great Depression, encouraging the flow of capital into other sectors of the economy. Similarly, on the Japanese side, during the Meiji restoration in the nineteenth century, massive public spending for railroads, highways, ports, and

communications facilities led the transition to the establishment
of a capitalist economy in Japan. Once again, as Japan faces
the ending of its postwar period of industrial recovery, there
is a great need for public expenditure in the Japanese
infrastructure. As the public investment of the Meiji
restoration prepared the way for Japan's emergence as a
capitalist economy, so the reconstruction of the domestic
infrastructure over the next few years can lead Japan's
entrance into the postindustrial age.

Such investment should occur in two broad areas: first,
in the distribution and communications networks for physical
goods, energy, and information, a development which will
contribute to the formation of a new market framework in
which price mechanisms will operate more fully in the economy;
and, second, in the basic urban facilities for social welfare -
for example, public hospitals, childcare centers, homes for the
aged, recreational facilities, and waste disposal systems.

These investments will have the substantial repercussive
effect of increasing the demand for such basic manufacturing
commodities as steel, chemical products, stone and clay, and
machinery. These basic manufacturing sectors were the core
of Japan's rapid growth after the war, and their capacities,
both soft and hard, still represent the mainstays of Japanese
manufacturing.(5) The investments will inevitably follow the
pattern of parallel development for a while. For example, new
distribution facilities will necessarily coexist with traditional
channels for several years, but they will prepare the
framework for new social and economic systems in Japan, in
addition to increasing the flexibility of the Japanese economy.
And above all, these investments offer a practicable line of
action for political leaders, since they will raise the quality of
daily life in Japan.

There will be opposition to such policies on fiscal and
financial grounds, but Japan needs very much to voluntarily
reduce its growth rate. This investment plan will accomplish
that goal by increasing the capital coefficient and by helping
to lower the savings ratio through the provision of greater
welfare security. Furthermore, if we are successful in
implementing the financial reforms proposed below, the
financial system will not impede Japan's gradual transformation
into a postindustrial economy.

Development of Energy Resources

Japan's access to the world's shrinking supply of energy (see
Table 9.3) is the major source of the economy's vulnerability,
and the reduction of this vulnerability and of the uncertainty
it engenders in the Japanese business community is absolutely
essential if Japan is to manage the multiple transitions it faces.

Table 9.3.   Net Imports of Oil
(in millions of barrels per day)

	1973	1974	1975	1976	1977	1978
United States	6.25	6.15	6.07	7.30	8.67	8.40
Japan	4.95	4.84	4.35	4.67	4.87	5.05

SOURCE: OECD Economic Outlook, no. 23, July 1978.

We must invest in the development of new energy sources and in the construction of facilities that will enable us to conserve energy in the future.   The parallel development strategy described above is directly applicable here as well; new energy development poses many alternatives, all of which contain elements of uncertainty regarding their practical applications, lead-times, and costs.   Under these circumstances, it would be dangerous as well as inefficient to single out one exclusive course of action.   Even though the strategy of parallel development is itself financially inefficient, we must use it as a mechanism to guarantee Japan's access to some sort of energy supply during critical shortages.   To that end, we must plan to use coal as a buffer energy, and to invest in foreign coal mining, transportation equipment, and coal utilization technologies, endeavors that will necessarily engage Japan in joint ventures with other economies.   And at the same time, we should seek to promote the so-called soft path of energy development.(6)   This approach would aim at the utilization of such untapped energy sources as solar energy, wind power, and terrestrial heat.

As in the case of public sector investment, the application of the strategy of parallel development to energy policy will be costly.   However, some increase in the capital coefficient of Japanese industry, far from being an obstacle to Japan's economic security, will help to assure the future stability of Japan's economy.   Furthermore, the additional cost of parallel energy development is estimated as approximately one dollar per month when distributed over the entire Japanese population, and this expenditure seems a reasonable price to pay for insurance against an energy shortage in the future.

Reform of the Financial System

The implementation of these strategies will depend upon yet another strategy - a thoroughgoing reform of the Japanese financial system. The financial sectors in Japan operate under the firm administrative control of the Ministry of Finance. Financial markets have been regulated by a number of institutional factors: entry into the subsectors of these markets is severely restricted by law or by administration, and most markets are segmented by institutional barriers that restrict the intersector mobility of capital. Also, interest rates are not determined by market forces but are either regulated by government policy or determined by bilateral bargaining between specific actors.

These mechanisms have permitted the strategic allocation of financial resources by the government to various sectors of the economy, and this system has definitely contributed to the rapid growth as well as to the reconstruction of the Japanese economy. Until now, the Japanese people have generally accepted these financial mechanisms because the reward of rapid income growth has compensated them for the low interest rates they have received on their savings accounts. However, this appears to be changing, and the current financial structure is becoming increasingly difficult to support. Discontent has grown over the fact that market factors cannot influence interest rates, and the absorption of national bonds on a large scale is becoming more and more difficult under the present system. Also, the foreign demand for Japanese currency has promoted the diversification of domestic capital, thus necessitating a reform of Japan's special financial system. And finally, the Bank of Japan has begun to shift the principal mechanism of its monetary control from lending policy to the operation of the bond market.

In contrast to the evolution of the present system, Japan's transition to a new economic order must be shaped in accordance with the wishes of the Japanese people; it must also open the door to a new international monetary flow. Therefore, the current very peculiar financial structure of Japan must give way to an "open and fair" system that utilizes market mechanisms and also includes provisions to cope with ill effects in the market. I propose the following policies as the first steps toward this reform:

1.   An open market for long- and short-term national bonds should be promoted by the removal of any restrictions on their interest rates; for example, national bonds and short-term government securities should be sold for tender, and the diversification of national bonds should be encouraged.

2. The determination of interest rates should be left, in principle, to the independent financial agencies. However, a floor interest rate should be established on small lot deposits in order to protect the small depositor.

3. Discriminatory codes that restrict entry into segments of the financial market should be abolished, and entry or merger decisions should be left to individual agencies, as long as they do not breach the antimonopoly laws.

Plan for Beef Importation(7)

Thus far in Japan, the liberalization of agricultural trade and the development of domestic agriculture have been treated as mutually exclusive goals. The limitation of agricultural imports represents one of the last bastions of protectionism in Japan, and, in particular, the restrictions on beef imports have become a focal point of the trade negotiations between Japan on the one side, and the United States, the EEC, and Oceania, on the other. I would argue, however, that the "conflict" between import liberalization and the development of the domestic beef industry can be resolved by the following allocation of the benefit that will arise from the importation of beef:

1. The present beef import quota should be abolished immediately, although it may be necessary to retain certain levels of tariff and import levy. This action will reduce the wholesale and retail prices of beef in Japan by one-half. Correspondingly, domestic beef consumption will rise from about 400,000 tons to a million tons annually (the price elasticity of beef demand is assumed at 1.5).

2. The decline in the income of domestic beef producers that will result from the decline in domestic prices can be compensated for by means of the deficiency payment scheme, already practiced in Japan for milk processing. The cost required for the deficiency payment for beef consumption is estimated at about 250 billion yen, and this cost will be almost exactly covered by the revenue from the beef tariff and import levy.

3. It is estimated that the benefit to the consumer as a result of simultaneous decline in prices and increase in consumption will amount to at least 500 billion yen per year, as measured by the

mechanism of the consumer surplus. In order
to pass some of this gain along to the domestic
beef industry, I propose a graduated income
tax, whose revenues could then be applied to
the promotion of the livestock industry through
pasture improvements and research and development.

4.   The increase in foreign exchange payments
brought about by this program will amount to
more than one billion U.S. dollars per year,
which will greatly contribute to the reduction
of Japan's export surplus.

5.   The beef trade liberalization program as described above should be carried out gradually
over a period of five to seven years to allow
for adjustment.

CONCLUSION

The above four policy designs are not offered as a comprehensive plan encompassing all sectors of the economy;
however, they can be regarded as the keystone for a whole
system of policy to lead Japan through the transition it
currently faces. Of course, many other areas of policy need
to be investigated individually in the evolution of new social
and economic structures in Japan - for example, transportation, urban renewal, regional reallocation, social welfare, and
related sociocultural developments. And in particular, the
study of new industrial formation is indispensable in the
determination of policy objectives for the future; new industries do not come into existence in a vacuum, but are
formulated in response to the needs described here and
elsewhere. We can discover new investment opportunities in
the process of meeting the challenges that presently confront
us: our current scarcities, restrictions, conflicts, and failures
can become the very sources from which innovation will flow in
the years ahead.

NOTES

(1)   According to Professor Harrod's equation, $gc = s(\Delta y/y$
$I/\Delta y - s/\Delta y)$, Japan's growth rate g will exceed that
of other economies so long as the Japanese savings ratio s
is high, assuming that the capital coefficient c, defining
the amount of investment required to gain additional
income, remains nearly equal between countries, as is
usual.

(2)   For more detailed discussions of Japanese corporate behavior, see, for example, the Spring-Summer 1978 issue
of   Japanese Economic Studies,   which   is   devoted   to
management and industry in Japan and contains the
following   articles: Kenichi   Imai,   "Japan's   Industrial
Organization";   Hideichiro   Nakamura,   "Japan,   Incor-
porated, and Postwar Democracy"; and Hiroshi Hagama,
"Characteristics of Japanese-Style Management."

(3)   The impact of "demand-pull" factors is supported by
American research as well; see, for example, a study
conducted on behalf of the U.S.-Japan Trade Council by
Wilbur F. Monro Associates, Inc., "Japanese Exports to
the United States: Analysis of 'Import-Pull' and 'Export-
Pull' Factors," June 1978.

(4)   These policy recommendations are based in part on the
policy proposals of the Forum for Policy Innovation, a
private,   nonpartisan,   nonprofit   voluntary   organization
begun in April 1976, which consists of a group of policy-
oriented social scientists in Japan.   The Forum aims to
offer   suggestions   for   the   future   design   of   Japanese
society and to identify opinions for viable policy systems
based   upon   empirical   studies   representing   a   wide
spectrum of views.

(5)   According   to   the   projections   of   the   Forum   for   Policy
Innovation, the investment plan will increase the capacity
utilization ratios of Japan's major manufacturing sectors in
the following way:

SECTOR	1977	1978	1979	1980
Steel	74.2	79.6	85.0	94.4% Utilized Capacity
Petro-Chemicals	76.9	80.8	84.6	92.3
Cement	62.9	67.2	71.3	76.4
Paper & Products	72.9	77.6	81.9	88.0
Aluminum	75.7	81.6	86.2	94.1

(6)   See A. Lovins, "Energy Strategy: The Road Not Taken?"
Foreign Affairs, October 1976, pp. 65-96.

(7)   This policy recommendation is based on the Forum for
Policy Innovation, "A Plan for Beef Import Liberalization
in Japan," Summary Press Release.

10 Preserving an Alliance: Recommendations in the Economic Sphere

Irving S. Friedman

Relations between Japan and the United States have been the subject of intense inquiry, particularly in recent years. This discussion has encompassed the political, diplomatic, and military aspects of the relationship between our two countries, as well as the economic issues of trade, exchange rates, balance of payments, capital movements, banking, and energy. It has also covered such social and cultural matters as communications, language, customs, religion, government, societal attitudes, and family life. Business and financial leaders have joined with politicians, academics, and other professionals in offering their views. The well-publicized Japanese reticence has given way to outpourings by Japanese commentators, not only on Japanese-American relations, but on Japan's role on the planet as well. Intellectual isolationism is no longer the order of the day in either the United States or Japan. As might be expected, some of the voices in this interchange have been strident, quarrelsome, and provocative; others have been calm, friendly, and reassuring.

Without this intellectual ferment, U.S.-Japanese relations would probably be greatly deteriorated today. Nevertheless, the ferment itself may, from time to time, have heightened concerns, fears, and misunderstandings. In order to refute the idea of an "unfair Japan" or an "unfair United States," it has occasionally been necessary to explain why this "unfair" image exists, and, unfortunately, the explanation that precedes the rebuttal may have made more of an impression upon the audience than the rebuttal itself. It should also be recognized that much of what is said about the "deterioration" of U.S.-Japanese relations is not based on actual events or policy declarations, but, rather, grows out of fears about what might happen, fears at times inspired by inaccurate or provocative statements. Nevertheless, the interchange between

116

the United States and Japan in recent years has produced
light as well as heat, and, on balance, the analyses and policy
recommendations that have emerged from this process, besides
being many and varied, have been useful, imaginative, and
practicable as well.

Neither country views the other as terra incognita any
longer. Americans today know a great deal more than ever
before about the details of our relations with the Japanese,
especially with respect to the economy. Questions involving
Japanese business behavior - for example, as it affects the
export of textiles, automobiles, electronics, and steel - have
been much more fully elucidated for the American public in
recent years. And just as Americans have a much better
understanding of Japanese industry, its strengths and
weaknesses, its needs and compulsions, the Japanese people
today know a great deal more about American industry,
agriculture, commerce, finance, labor, and politics. Each
country appreciates not only the strengths of the other, but
also its difficulties and constraints. These include problems of
employment, growth rates, environment, natural resource
availability, inflation, balance of payments, exchange rates,
and limitations on monetary, fiscal, and investment policies.

Both countries are currently experiencing problems in all
of these areas, although, of course, the nature and extent of
each nation's difficulties vary. Diplomacy often obscures the
keen awareness of these problems, but the awareness is there
and it influences leaders in the public and private sectors of
Japan and the United States. The extent to which information
about each country is available in the other should be stressed
because this sort of interchange is relatively new in United
States-Japanese relations. Leaders in both countries now
enjoy unprecedented access to analyses of the other's
corporate structure and capital formation, fiscal and monetary
policies, role in the world market, and patterns of public and
private consumption. As a veteran of the period when each
country was something of a mystery to the other, I am indeed
envious of the knowledge base now available to Japanese and
American policy makers.

In the interest of strengthening relations between Japan
and the United States, it is imperative that these relations be
regarded unabashedly within the context of a military and
political alliance. Terms like "partnership" and "collaboration"
should be eschewed in considering the interaction between
Japan and the United States: they imply too much or too little.
It is in the national interest of each country to regard itself
as the ally of the other. We should not be reluctant to
proclaim this relationship in such terms, for the constant
recognition of an alliance between Japan and the United States
would enable both nations to keep in perspective the fact that
their current differences, although surely not negligible, are
far less important than their need for each other.

Both countries are strong, huge, industrial, market-oriented economies with high incomes and worldwide interests. They have both shown a great capacity for structural change, and are both very influential in the spheres of world trade, services, and finance. Their chief economic dissimilarities lie in the areas of natural resources and government-business relations. At the moment, Japan has a large current account surplus in its balance of payments, the United States, a large deficit. Until recently, the dollar was weak in foreign exchange markets and the yen, strong. These temporary differences have tremendously colored recent thinking on both sides of the Pacific, often causing more fundamental matters to be virtually ignored.

It is in the national interest of both the United States and Japan to preserve the multilateral trade and payments system. Both have an interest in promoting prosperous and more stable conditions in the developing countries. However, it is natural to expect that Japan and the United States will not pursue identical policies with respect to such matters as energy, foreign investment, capital inflows, and technology transfer. The existence of an alliance does not presuppose the elimination of all dissimilarity, friction, and competition. It does, however, presuppose that the solutions to disagreements and the national responses to competitive situations will be conditioned by the strong common desire to preserve the alliance. Keen competition with one's ally is, after all, compatible with the eagerness to see the ally prosper.

What is most important about the alliance relationship is that it serves as a framework for modulating responses that might damage the fundamental ties between nations. The existence of an alliance acts as a check upon reactions that cause suspicion and "scapegoatism," and upon protective or punitive measures that could bring relations to the brink of economic warfare. An ally considers the strategic resource needs of its partner as vital to itself. It does not allow financial considerations to weaken relations based upon political and military needs. It makes certain that the costs as well as the benefits of the alliance are shared in a manner which both sides deem reasonable (if not always wholly satisfactory). It does all that is feasible to avoid taking actions that affect the other ally significantly without prior consultation. It gives the highest priority to reconciling this relationship with its system of other alliances. An ally must constantly reassess the substance of the relationship to ensure its continuing relevancy to changing global conditions, but always with a view to perpetuating the alliance. It recognizes that such alliances reduce and constrain a nation's freedom of action in several spheres - including the economic one - and it freely accepts such constraints as more than offset by the benefits of the alliance.

Alliance relations, as translated into action by people and institutions, differ from one nation to the next. With respect to economic relations, each ally should be sensitive to the economic needs of its counterpart, and should consider all differences within the framework of their common interests. This holds true whether the problems involve exchange rates, foreign trade, business practices, capital flows, monetary systems, international finance, or relations with other countries - in the case of the United States and Japan, such regions as China, the Soviet Union, and Southeast Asia.

Because allies can never share similar policies on all questions, it is misleading, frustrating, and corrosive to view every difference in policy as a sign of the impending deterioration of the alliance. Occasionally, the United States and Japan may follow the same policies, but such congruence should arise from the congruence of their national interests in these areas, and not from the fact that one ally has persuaded, coerced, or bullied the other into pursuing the same line of action. It is, of course, possible for one ally to win such victories over the other, but these victories are Pyrrhic ones as far as the fate of the alliance is concerned.

In the case of U.S.-Japanese relations, one example of alliance diplomacy concerns the question of the yen/dollar exchange rate. Japan prospered mightily during the period of a stable exchange rate in the 1950s and 1960s. That period saw many problems in the areas of exchange and trade restrictions, business practices, controls on financial inflows, foreign investment regulations, and so forth. Despite these problems, all viewed the stable exchange rate as a factor that encouraged Japanese investment and growth. Today many Japanese experts favor a return to stable yen/dollar rates. They point to the low levels of investment in the 1970s in contrast to the high levels in the 1950s and 1960s, when investments were channelled into productive industries and the Japanese "miracle" became the object of worldwide praise and envy. These experts believe that the stable exchange rate was part of the environment in which this progress was made.

The exact truth is not so certain. The extent to which exchange rate stability really contributed to Japan's postwar growth can be debated ad infinitum; similarly, it is not clear how much the current volatility in exchange rates has influenced the decrease in the level of investment in Japan and other industrial nations. What is clear, however, is the fact that the issue of competitive exchange rates did not significantly affect relations between Japan and the United States a decade ago, even though Japanese exports were zooming and the exchange rate favored Japanese exporters.

My own conviction is that the exchange rate did not arouse controversy at the time, not because it was deemed economically valid, but simply because this rate had been

internationally determined in the first place. In an era of
floating rates, the likelihood is much greater that exchange
rate changes will create the suspicion of self-serving and
unfair practices on the part of one country or another. Such
charges are being heard repeatedly nowadays; currency value
fluctuation is too obvious a scapegoat to be ignored by those
hurt by international competition, particularly as countries
continue to intervene in exchange markets. These fears are
not new: anxiety over rate manipulation was so strong
throughout the world during the 1930s that it inspired the
formation of the International Monetary Fund after the war.

A stable yen/dollar rate would serve the alliance
relationship between Japan and the United States much better
than the current floating rate does, simply because it would
eliminate this source of friction and suspicion, and encourage
closer cooperation between the United States and Japan in
economic matters. By itself, of course, this premise does not
render the move to a stable rate economically feasible or wise,
since monetary and economic conditions differ widely between
the two countries. But the fact that a stable rate would
greatly improve Japanese-American relations should certainly
constitute a strong argument to both nations for examining the
preconditions for exchange rate stability, and, if possible,
acting when they are met. If the yen depreciates in relation
to the dollar, the matter will become more urgent. If the
United States enters a recession while the Japanese export
movement remains strong, and the United States continues its
current account deficit while the Japanese enjoy a surplus,
the depreciation of the yen could well evoke accusations of
competitive manipulation and demands for countermeasures.
For, whereas the depreciation of the dollar could be viewed as
assisting the "adjustment" process in rectifying the American
trade balance, the depreciation of the yen damages this
adjustment and impedes the efforts of Japanese monetary and
fiscal authorities to combat inflation as well.

In the early 1980s, both countries could, on balance,
profit by stabilizing the yen/dollar rate despite the obvious
disparities in their respective inflation and interest rates; I
believe that they will indeed move toward stabilization. At the
very least, it should be made clear that, whatever exchange
rate policy is followed, both the United States and Japan must
agree on its fairness and appropriateness. And this action
must take place before the exchange rate issue blows up.

Having proposed that both nations regard all their
relations as occurring within the framework of an alliance, and
having suggested one area in which the alliance relationship
might be implemented - an area in which it needs to be
implemented soon - I would like to offer several further
suggestions regarding various forms of economic collaboration
which the United States and Japan might consider in the spirit
of alliance relations.

Defense Costs(1)

The current distribution of defense costs between Japan and the United States is based on three key assumptions: 1) The cost of the American presence in Japan is the focal point of defense cost calculations; 2) the Japanese contribution to this defense force is chiefly economic and involves no substitution of Japanese for American military personnel; and 3) as a Far Eastern country, Japan is protected under the Far Eastern component of the American military umbrella. This final premise in particular needs to be fundamentally reexamined. Japan is a global economy. It imports resources from all over the world. Political disturbances anywhere on the globe adversely affect Japan. It would seem, therefore, that the entire U.S.-NATO military constellation protects Japan, and not simply its Far Eastern component.

Japan's economy is clearly able to support a much larger defense effort. Leaving aside the military-political question of how Japan might actually assume a share of the defense burden commensurate to its economic strength and security needs, a true alliance between the United States and Japan would certainly require greater parity between the American and Japanese contributions to a defense system that protects them both equally, although the content of these contributions would presumably differ greatly.

Resource Availability

The Japanese need desperately to insure their supply of fuel and other raw materials, and also need America's guarantee that Japan will not be crippled by the lack of such resources. It is not in the true spirit of alliance for each country to measure its relative dependency only in terms of its own needs. Those of us who experienced World War II learned that we could not divorce ourselves from the resource vulnerabilities of our allies, nor could they divorce themselves from ours. The United States can guarantee Japan's access to those resources which Japan obtains from us, and, in the cases of other materials, the United States can help Japan obtain supplies from Canada, Mexico, or other friendly countries. This kind of activity would in a sense increase Japan's dependency on the United States, but it would not add to Japan's dependency elsewhere, and it naturally assumes that Japan would rather rely on the United States than on nations with which it is not allied. Both nations should reinforce the efforts already begun along these lines by infusing them with the spirit of alliance rather than basing them on such narrower considerations as balance-of-payments behavior. Our two countries must approach the energy problem with each other in mind, for, in fact, a less coordinated energy policy could ultimately destroy the alliance.

Barriers to Trade and Capital Movements

Much more remains to be done in the areas of trade and capital flow barriers to end the current atmosphere of confrontation, which at times borders on outright hostility. In both countries, the most rational solution would be the immediate removal of all restrictions to trade and capital movement. But although such an action would be in the best national interest of each country, special interests within each would be temporarily hurt. Since both countries are political democracies, they must both find ways of responding to individual sectors that manage to harmonize the national interest with special interests.

As a beginning, both the American and the Japanese publics should be enlightened with respect to the nature and extent of existing barriers to trade and capital movements. The present credibility gap should be closed and differences in trade practices should be explained, with particular reference to the specific interests that would be adversely affected by further liberalization. Public opinion in either country may find it easier to tolerate the protective actions of the other government if these actions are justified in precise terms rather than being obscured by diplomatic rhetoric and aggregate figures. Also, as I suggest below, negotiations for the reduction and removal of barriers to trade and capital movements would best be conducted within the framework of international institutions. Within such contexts, special "bargaining" between Japan and the United States would inevitably continue, but it would take place in a calmer, more reasonable atmosphere.

The agenda for cooperation within the framework of the U.S.-Japanese alliance could conceivably include many other items as well. In addition to those mentioned above, health and education, cultural exchange, and space exploration might be singled out as particularly promising areas for collaboration. It would be of tremendous benefit to the rest of the world if Japan were to join the United States in major research and development efforts in the area of health care. To some extent, Japan already supports such activities, but it could easily expand its present contribution. Similarly, as an ally and an advanced industrial power, would Japan not be a worthy collaborator with the United States in the exploration of space? This collaboration, if deemed appropriate, could include research and development as well as actual participation in space flights. If the cost sharing were based upon each country's relative benefit and ability to sustain expenses, the Japanese would take upon themselves a major share in the management decisions of the space program. Finally, although much has been done in recent years in the area of cultural exchange, these efforts are slight when compared to the need for them and the benefit to be derived from them. Japanese language studies for Americans could be promoted both in Japan and in the United States, combined with opportunities for visitor exchange and English language study for Japanese. Also, the success of the Japan Today program in the United States could be matched by a United States Today program in Japan.

Other areas, such as the law of the seas, development finance, international monetary systems, environmental protection, and population distribution might also lend themselves to more collaborative endeavors on the part of the United States and Japan. If we assume the continued existence of an alliance between two such extraordinary nations, both with global interests and enormous economic capacities, the opportunities for new initiatives and approaches will multiply as individuals with different backgrounds become aware of the potential for cooperation.

It must be kept in mind, however, that each country is indeed a global power, and is therefore engaged in other major international relationships, of which the U.S.-NATO connection is a prime example. Both Japan and the United States need a multilateral trading system. Bilateralism is, after all, only an exaggerated form of protectionism and is incompatible with national interests which are worldwide in scope. Therefore, both countries must recognize their common need to strengthen global codes and institutions, such as the International Monetary Fund, the World Bank, and GATT. This does not mean that they must always agree when they meet within these institutions. However, they can and should agree that their own national policies - including their bilateral relations - will be conducted within a multilateral framework, and that they will use these multilateral institutions as mechanisms for dealing with issues that affect their relations with each other.

The United States and Japan must find mutually satisfactory solutions to their "bilateral" problems - matters such as the American deficit/Japanese surplus, and the exchange rate level. These solutions must also take into account the fact that both nations are involved with other countries as well. For example, the exclusion of an Icelandic or Brazilian export from either the American or the Japanese market in the interests of U.S.-Japanese bilateralism represents an unstable and inequitable solution to the problem. Similarly, if Japan "helps" the United States by acting in a manner that Canada or the Philippines perceives as unfair, the action is likely to prove unstable, even if it does temporarily resolve a particular complaint. Most Favored Nation clauses help to some extent, but not always and not fully, particularly if they are viewed as de facto forms of protectionism arising from bilateral deals in which the interests of other nations are slighted. Alliance relations require each ally to walk a tightrope of special and often secret communications and understandings with its partner, without falling into the abyss of unfair collusion and jeopardizing relations with friendly countries. (See Tables 10.1, 10.2, 10.3, and 10.4 for an analysis of the multilateral character of the Japanese and American trade structures.)

My recommendation is that this dilemma is best resolved when the actions of both allies conform to the agreed-upon international codes of behavior administered by international institutions and when the two nations discuss their problems and settle their differences within the forums of these institutions. At this time, agreements are being sought that will strengthen GATT in the future, and this endeavor offers the United States and Japan another opportunity to demonstrate their support for this multilateral institution. Proposals to strengthen the World Bank, the Asian Development Bank (ADB), the Inter-American Development Bank (IDB) and other organizations provide additional chances to display these broader concerns. Multilateral institutions also afford the opportunity to defuse potentially explosive issues, such as the fluctuations in the dollar/yen rate or the restrictions on trade and capital movements. My own experience in heading IMF consultation teams with Japan for many years convinced me that it is indeed possible for an international staff to deal quietly and effectively with delicate issues within the framework of internationally accepted and universally applicable codes of behavior. In this respect, GATT is weak when compared to the IMF and the World Bank. A reinforced consultative machinery within GATT could provide the method for removing certain U.S.-Japanese issues from the atmosphere of confrontation induced by bilateral negotiations. If these questions were handled on a continuing basis with the help of an international staff, "confrontations" would then occur only between a single nation's priorities and constraints, on the one hand, and the internationally accepted code of behavior, on the other.

It might well be argued that the "alliance" arrangement is not the only possible approach to U.S.-Japanese relations. After all, alliances are the exceptions, rather than the rules, of international affairs. But for reasons that could be elaborated in detail, and which I have very briefly sketched above, I believe that both the United States and Japan are best served by treating their relationship as an alliance. The United States already includes other major industrial competitors among its closest allies. The strains and stresses of competition, national differences, and structural adjustments create tensions which, at times, may threaten these various

Table 10.1
The Multilateral Character of Japan's Export Trade
(Japan's 20 Largest Trading Partners)

	1971		1975		1976		1977		1978	
	Mil. $	%	Mil. $	%	Mil. $	%	Mil. $	%	Mil. $	%
Japan's Exports, total	24,081	100.0	55,728	100.0	67,320	100.0	81,125	100.0	98,415	100.0
Sold to:										
USA	7,617	31.6	11,242	20.2	15,923	23.6	20,077	24.7	25,357	25.8
Korea	857	3.6	2,246	4.0	2,828	4.2	4,113	5.1	6,056	6.1
West Germany	659	2.7	1,660	3.0	2,245	3.3	2,802	3.4	3,684	3.7
Taiwan	925	3.8	1,820	3.3	2,283	3.4	2,574	3.2	3,615	3.7
Saudi Arabia	137	0.6	1,350	2.4	1,892	2.8	2,364	2.9	3,284	3.3
Australia	721	3.0	1,738	3.1	2,313	3.4	2,347	2.9	2,718	2.8
Hong Kong	789	3.3	1,377	2.5	1,843	2.7	2,339	2.9	3,112	3.2
UK	575	2.4	1,472	2.6	1,401	2.1	1,964	2.4	2,361	2.4
Iran	238	1.0	1,853	3.3	1,709	2.5	1,942	2.4	2,719	2.8
Indonesia	454	1.9	1,849	3.3	1,641	2.4	1,812	2.2	2,114	2.1
Singapore	509	2.1	1,522	2.7	1,533	2.3	1,732	2.1	2,345	2.4
Canada	878	3.6	1,151	2.1	1,554	2.3	1,721	2.1	1,888	1.9
Thailand	446	1.8	958	1.7	1,072	1.6	1,370	1.7	1,541	1.6
Panama	236	1.0	1,113	0.2	1,306	1.9	1,339	1.6	1,467	1.5
Netherlands	362	1.5	726	1.3	1,088	1.6	1,316	1.6	1,613	1.6
Philippines	465	1.9	1,026	1.8	1,115	1.7	1,108	1.4	1,559	1.6
Greece	254	1.0	336	0.6	744	1.1	1,104	1.4	901	0.9
France	192	0.8	700	1.3	968	1.4	1,023	1.3	1,116	1.1
Nigeria	96	0.4	585	1.0	574	0.8	1,017	1.2	963	1.0
Kuwait	82	0.3	367	0.7	720	1.1	942	1.2	781	0.8
China	579	2.4	2,258	4.0	1,666	2.5	1,955	2.4	3,074	3.1
USSR	378	1.6	1,626	2.9	2,254	3.3	1,951	2.4	2,529	2.6

SOURCE: International Monetary Fund, Direction of Trade, Annual 1971-77, and Yearbook 1979, Washington, D.C., 1979.

Table 10.2
The Multilateral Character of Japan's Import Trade
(Japan's 20 Largest Trading Partners)

Japan's Imports, total	1971 Mil. $ 19,773	% 100.0	1975 Mil. $ 57,846	% 100.0	1976 Mil. $ 64,891	% 100.0	1977 Mil. $ 71,325	% 100.0	1978 Mil. $ 79,900	% 100.0
Bought from:										
USA	5,002	25.3	11,618	20.1	11,865	18.3	12,474	17.5	14,929	18.7
Saudi Arabia	753	3.8	6,131	10.6	7,836	12.1	8,570	12.0	8,503	10.6
Australia	1,753	8.9	4,154	7.2	5,369	8.3	5,326	7.5	5,340	6.7
Indonesia	855	4.3	3,430	5.9	4,096	6.3	5,033	7.1	5,284	6.6
Iran	1,365	6.9	4,978	8.6	4,454	6.9	4,269	6.0	4,256	5.3
Canada	1,005	5.1	2,498	4.3	2,719	4.2	2,894	4.1	3,206	4.0
UAE	229	1.2	1,774	3.1	2,472	3.8	2,769	3.9	2,639	3.3
Kuwait	417	2.1	2,010	3.5	2,017	3.1	2,502	3.5	2,501	3.1
Korea	273	1.4	1,307	2.3	1,919	2.9	2,160	3.0	2,630	3.3
Malaysia	374	1.9	691	1.2	1,364	2.1	1,579	2.2	1,911	2.4
West Germany	609	3.1	1,139	2.0	1,230	1.9	1,507	2.1	2,011	2.5
Brunei	36	0.2	1,021	1.8	1,216	1.9	1,431	2.0	1,403	1.8
Taiwan	288	1.5	811	1.4	1,192	1.8	1,297	1.8	1,764	2.2
UK	418	2.1	810	1.4	845	1.3	966	1.3	1,391	1.7
Brazil	223	1.1	882	1.5	819	1.3	953	1.3	790	1.0
South Africa	318	1.6	880	1.5	763	1.2	909	1.3	1,063	1.3
Philippines	516	2.6	1,120	1.9	794	1.2	904	1.3	1,066	1.3
Oman	81	0.4	520	0.9	684	1.0	890	1.2	909	1.1
India	377	1.9	658	1.1	802	1.2	806	1.1	799	1.1
Thailand	231	1.2	723	1.2	849	1.3	754	1.1	849	1.2
China	322	1.6	1,529	2.6	1,373	2.1	1,560	2.2	2,045	2.9
USSR	497	2.5	1,169	2.0	1,169	1.8	1,433	2.0	1,453	2.0

SOURCE: International Monetary Fund, Direction of Trade, Annual 1971-77, and Yearbook 1979, Washington, D.C., 1979.

Table 10.3
The Multilateral Character of United States Export Trade
(The United States' 20 Largest Trading Partners)

US Exports, total	1971 Mil. $ 44,137	% 100.0	1975 Mil. $ 107,586	% 100.0	1976 Mil. $ 115,006	% 100.0	1977 Mil. $ 121,238	% 100.0	1978 Mil. $ 143,660	% 100.0
Sold to:										
Canada	10,365	23.5	21,744	20.2	24,109	21.0	25,788	21.3	28,372	19.7
Japan	4,055	9.2	9,563	8.9	10,144	8.8	10,529	8.7	12,885	9.0
West Germany	2,831	6.4	5,194	4.8	5,730	5.0	5,989	4.9	6,957	4.8
UK	2,369	5.4	4,527	4.2	4,799	4.2	5,951	4.9	7,119	5.0
Mexico	1,620	3.7	5,141	4.8	4,990	4.3	4,821	4.0	6,680	4.6
Netherlands	1,786	4.0	4,194	3.9	4,645	4.0	4,812	4.0	5,683	4.0
Saudi Arabia	164	0.4	1,502	1.4	2,774	2.4	3,575	3.0	4,370	3.0
France	1,373	3.1	3,031	2.8	3,449	3.0	3,503	2.9	4,167	2.9
Venezuela	787	1.8	2,243	2.1	2,628	2.3	3,171	2.6	3,727	2.6
Belgium	1,077	2.4	2,417	2.2	2,991	2.6	3,137	2.6	3,653	2.5
Italy	1,314	3.0	2,867	2.7	3,068	2.7	2,789	2.3	3,360	2.3
Iran	482	1.1	3,244	3.0	2,776	2.4	2,731	2.3	3,684	2.6
Brazil	966	2.2	3,056	2.8	2,809	2.4	2,490	2.1	2,978	2.1
Korea	681	1.5	1,762	1.6	2,015	1.7	2,371	2.0	3,160	2.2
Australia	1,004	2.3	1,815	1.7	2,185	1.9	2,356	1.9	2,910	2.0
Spain	651	1.5	2,228	2.1	2,088	1.8	1,955	1.6	1,975	1.4
Taiwan	510	1.2	1,659	1.5	1,635	1.4	1,798	1.5	2,339	1.6
Israel	707	1.6	1,551	1.4	1,409	1.2	1,446	1.2	1,926	1.3
Switzerland	627	1.4	1,153	1.1	1,173	1.0	1,749	1.4	1,733	1.2
Hong Kong	424	1.0	808	0.7	1,115	1.0	1,291	1.1	1,625	1.1
USSR	162	0.4	1,836	1.7	2,308	2.0	1,627	1.3	2,252	1.6
China	--	--	304	0.2	135	0.1	171	0.1	824	0.6

SOURCE: International Monetary Fund, Direction of Trade, Annual 1971-77, and Yearbook 1979, Washington, D.C., 1979.

Table 10.4
The Multilateral Character of United States Import Trade
(The United States' 20 Largest Trading Partners)

US Imports, total	1971 Mil. $ 48,355	% 100.0	1975 Mil. $ 103,417	% 100.0	1976 Mil. $ 129,566	% 100.0	1977 Mil. $ 157,546	% 100.0	1978 Mil. $ 183,136	% 100.0
Bought from:										
Canada	13,466	27.8	22,752	22.0	27,565	21.3	30,868	19.6	34,645	18.9
Japan	7,702	15.9	12,336	11.9	16,922	13.1	20,195	12.8	26,462	14.4
Germany	3,874	8.0	5,750	5.6	5,965	4.6	7,691	4.9	10,562	5.8
Saudi Arabia	105	0.2	2,987	2.9	5,847	4.5	6,998	4.4	5,819	3.2
Nigeria	138	0.3	3,525	3.4	5,251	4.0	6,499	4.1	4,977	2.7
UK	2,651	5.5	4,047	3.9	4,545	3.5	5,465	3.5	6,921	3.8
Mexico	1,339	2.8	3,112	3.0	3,655	2.8	4,769	3.0	6,195	3.4
Venezuela	1,291	2.7	3,869	3.7	3,782	2.9	4,285	2.7	3,738	2.0
Taiwan	867	1.8	2,162	2.1	3,298	2.5	4,036	2.6	5,695	3.1
Libya	54	0.1	1,120	1.1	2,406	1.9	4,043	2.6	3,993	2.2
Indonesia	220	0.4	2,447	2.4	3,277	2.5	3,738	2.4	3,884	2.1
Italy	1,491	3.1	2,641	2.6	2,721	2.1	3,281	2.1	4,468	2.4
France	1,155	2.4	2,281	2.2	2,669	2.1	3,247	2.1	4,347	2.4
Algeria	21	0.0	1,448	1.4	2,344	1.8	3,270	2.1	3,698	2.0
Korea	491	1.0	1,586	1.5	2,646	2.0	3,162	2.0	4,087	2.2
Hong Kong	1,051	2.2	1,734	1.7	2,636	2.0	3,133	2.0	3,764	2.1
Iran	144	0.3	1,579	1.5	1,631	1.3	3,045	1.9	3,164	1.7
Brazil	808	1.7	1,623	1.6	1,888	1.5	2,385	1.5	3,035	1.7
UAE	93	0.2	781	0.8	1,532	1.2	1,824	1.2	2,030	1.1
Trinidad & Tobago	228	0.5	1,228	1.2	1,571	1.2	1,748	1.1	1,482	0.8
Poland	114	0.2	263	0.2	339	0.3	355	0.2	479	0.3
USSR	61	0.1	280	0.3	239	0.2	469	0.3	561	0.3
China	5	0.0	171	0.2	222	0.2	223	0.1	356	0.2

SOURCE: International Monetary Fund, Direction of Trade, Annual 1971-77, and Yearbook 1979, Washington, D.C., 1979.

alliance relationships. Alliances do not end tensions; in many ways, they create additional ones. But they exist because the ends they serve are regarded as overwhelmingly important, and unquestionably worth whatever tensions they may cause.

A nation cannot sustain an alliance relationship if it allows itself to become preoccupied with parochial concerns, or if it loses sight of the overarching goals of world peace, world order, and the preservation of human life and culture. The elevation of the U.S.-Japanese relationship to the level of an alliance offers the assurance that national rather than special interests will ultimately prevail. It may be argued that relations between Japan and the United States today differ significantly from the behavior that characterizes an alliance. These differences have prompted the expression of my concern here. We need to take stock of this situation and to avert its consequences while we still have the opportunity to do so.

Index

About the
Contributors

DIANE TASCA served as Rapporteur/Editor for the U.S-Japan
Study Group at the Lehrman Institute. Before joining the
Institute in 1978 as the Assistant for Special Projects, Ms.
Tasca contributed to several publications in the area of public
health at the University of Michigan. She holds a doctorate
in English Literature from the University of Illinois.

ZYGMUNT NAGORSKI, Vice-President of the Lehrman Institute
and Special Advisor to the Aspen Institute for Humanistic
Studies, spent ten years with the Council on Foreign
Relations as its Program Director. Prior to that, he was a
Foreign Service officer, and his duties included assignments
in South Korea, Egypt, and France. His publications include
The Psychology of East-West Trade, along with a monthly
column in Money Manager, a specialized Wall Street periodical,
and frequent contributions to the New York Times, Wall
Street Journal, and other periodicals and newspapers.

MASAHISA NAITOH, educated as an attorney, has served in
numerous capacities within the Japanese Ministry of
International Trade and Industry (MITI), where he has been
involved in setting policy in such areas as consumer
protection, industrial organization, and export credit. He
has also written numerous articles on industrial policy and
has coauthored Competition and Monopoly. In his capacity as
Special Trade Representative of MITI, a position which he
held from 1975 to 1979, Mr. Naitoh played a large role in the
United States-Japanese trade negotiations. In 1979, he
assumed his new position as Director of the Americas-Oceania
Division of MITI in Tokyo.